THE PSYCHOLOGY OF COUNSELLING

Eleanor O'Leary

M.A., Ph.D., H.D.E., A.B.Ps.S.

The Psychology

of

Counselling

CORK UNIVERSITY PRESS

First Published 1982 at the Cork University Press,
University College Cork, Ireland.

ISBN 0 902561 22 7

Set in 10 on 11pt Press Roman by Graphica Ltd.,
Produced and printed in Ireland by Printplan & Associates Limited

To my professor and friend,
Dr. Peter Dempsey
of the Department of Applied Psychology, U.C.C.

Acknowledgements

I am deeply indebted to the following:

Professor Peter Dempsey, who advised on this work at all stages of its development.

Fr. Brian Kelly, whose unfailing encouragement and critical assistance have been invaluable.

Professor Don Wallis, U.W.I.S.T., Cardiff, for his great courtesy and helpfulness.

Dr. Christopher Simms, Dept. of Psychology, U.C.D. for his observations.

Miss Elizabeth Dunne, Dept. of Applied Psychology, U.C.C. and to Mrs. Anna Lenahan and Mr. John McCarthy of the same Department, friends in need and in deed.

Professors Carl Rogers, G.T. Barrett-Lennard, E. M. Berger and R.E. Bills for their kindness and the inspiration of their writings and to all those others whose books or articles have promoted my understanding of counselling.

Sandra Fisher, Deirdre Mangan and Catherine Ryan for their assistance with the text.

The Guidance Counsellors in the Cork area and their students.

Finally I must pay special thanks to my dear parents, John and Joan O'Leary, to the other members of my family, to the sisters of my community in the Mercy Convent, Kinsale, and to my friends.

Contents

CHAPTER 4 CORE OUTCOMES: THEORY AND RESEARCH

CHAPTER 5 MEASUREMENT OF CORE CONDITIONS AND CORE OUTCOMES

Foreword

It is a great pleasure to contribute a foreword to this study of *The Psychology of Counselling* by Dr. Eleanor O'Leary, Director of the Counselling/Guidance Course in University College Cork and member of the National Executive of the Guidance Counsellors Association of Ireland. It is a book combining practical injunction with a clear exposition of theoretical fundamentals and an empirical investigation of the most significant factors in the counselling relationship.

The author has called her book *The Psychology of Counselling* implying that she treats of the most essential psychological issues involved in counselling, especially client-centred or person-centred counselling—in the tradition of Professor Carl Rogers and his associates. The claim is a fair one since the work discusses the nature of counselling, the main approaches thereto, its techniques and goals, the core conditions of empathy, congruence, level of regard and unconditionality, and the core concepts of the self, ideal self and self-acceptance. Subsequent to this discussion the author describes three measuring instruments, Barrett-Lennard's Relationship Inventory, Bills' Index of Adjustment and Values and Berger's Acceptance of Self and Others Scale, assesses their validity and reliability and applies them to groups of adolescents in the school situation. The investigation leads to the conclusion that while all the various conditions mentioned previously are important, the factors of empathy and self-acceptance emerge as having a certain priority operationally. This has implications for diagnosis and treatment as well as for the selection and training of counsellors.

Counselling and Guidance as a discipline has close links not only with clinical but with educational and occupational psychology. Many of those who come for help have problems of adjustment and/or of occupational/educational choice. The difficulties presenting themselves have simultaneously mental health, educational or occupational dimensions. This would seem to indicate that at under-graduate or post-graduate level, exposure to the problems, concepts and techniques of the main applied fields should be included in the

11

training of students of psychology. As would-be scientists as well as would-be professionals they should also be taught the varieties of systematic observation and experimentation, whether directed towards the behaviour and experience of other individuals and groups or of themselves.

The concept of the self as a basic one not alone in the person-centred approach to counselling and guidance but in the entire discipline of psychology and indeed in human living. I have found it convenient to think of the self in terms of a fourfold framework, a body self, a social self, a cognitive self and an affective self. Through the skill of the counsellor, an adolescent or an adult learns to accept his body—and to be at home in it. He comes to know of his need for recognition, of the roles he plays, the norms, the standards, the ideals he accepts or rejects. He learns that he needs meaning and can grasp meaning, reflect upon himself, understand his understanding, and be receptive of insight. He becomes aware of the vast deep world of his feelings, emotions, desires and of the defences he has erected against them. He becomes conscious of his power to choose, to decide, to commit himself, of his capacity to scrutinise the past, to confront the challenge of present and future circumstances, and thus to create himself in freedom.

Understanding love and loving understanding conduce to self-awareness, self-acceptance and self-possession. It establishes people in their human freedom and their human dignity. In our technological and ideological age when human dignity is so often abused and human freedom so often suppressed, I believe that enlightened skilful counselling can do much to promote the healing and liberation of man. This book will help in the attainment of that end.

P. J. R. Dempsey,
Professor of Applied Psychology,
University College, Cork, Ireland   December 15, 1981

1

Counselling: *Nature and Approaches*

1.1 The Nature of Counselling

Counselling belongs within the context of helping relationships in which, according to Rogers (1958), at least one of the parties has the intention of promoting the growth, development, maturity, improved functioning and improved ability to cope with the life of the other.

Counselling may also be described as an encounter through which a client is afforded healing help, leading to the diminution or solution of the personal adjustment problems which beset him, as well as to positive growth and actualisation of his personality. It is an encounter between a counsellor and client taking the form of a counselling interview. The counsellor neither commands nor forbids, neither exhorts, advises nor intellectually interprets symptoms. Rather he affords the client an opportunity to explore his difficulties and the attitudes which surround them. As a result of this exploration, the client gains an understanding of himself which brings his behaviour within the sphere of his conscious control and enables him to take positive steps in new directions in the light of his new orientation. The counsellor's function in this process is not to offer a solution to the client's problems, but to assist the client to see himself more clearly in all his positive, negative and contradictory aspects. This self-awareness and self-understanding is the essence of therapeutic insight.

This viewpoint is consonant with client-centred counselling which is one of the three main approaches and techniques encountered in counselling and therapy today. It is most sharply divergent from behavioural theory and techniques. It differs also from psychoanalytic theory and practice although belonging within the psychodynamic orientation to adjustment problems. It is appropriate to discuss briefly the theory and techniques of the behavioural and psychoanalytic schools before considering the client-centred counselling and therapy tradition within which this research is centred.

1.2 The Behavioural Approach and Technique

The behavioural approach and technique is derived from the work of

Pavlov and Watson on classical conditioning and that of Skinner on operant conditioning. The goal of the behaviour therapies is to reduce or eliminate maladaptive learned behaviours. In its original formulation, behaviour therapy did not consider it necessary to delve into the specific origin of problem behaviour. This traditional view has been significantly modified in more recent theory and research in behaviour psychotherapy.

A central idea in the therapies based on operant conditioning techniques is that of reinforcement. Any manipulation or event that increases the probability that a given response will be made is a reinforcement. Depression is a condition often treated by behaviour modification procedures. Depressed people, for example, may acquire self-debasing attitudes through having been exposed to negative rather than positive reinforcement earlier in their lives. Using learning principles to modify depression, the patient's self-concept may be strengthened by reinforcing him — with praise or whatever else he values — when he acts on his own initiative.

In operant conditioning techniques, the choice of the reinforcement is vital. Stimuli that are meaningless or irrelevant to the subject cannot effectively modify his behaviour. Often, the major clinical task is identifying the reinforcer that will work. For example, social reinforcers (approval of others, friendliness) may be very powerful stimuli for some individuals but not for others. In addition, the reinforcer will not be effective unless the subject understands that the reinforcement is dependent upon the desired response. It was this growing awareness of (a) the importance of the meaning of the reinforcer to the individual and (b) the importance of the client's understanding of the principles upon which the therapist's programme was based which eventually brought behavioural psychotherapy very much closer to the client-centred model

Behaviour psychotherapy is a systematic technique for designing a programme to deal with problem behaviour of a particular kind. It is most appropriately used with neuroses. Marzillier (1978) points out that it matters little whether the method used to effect change is essentially a verbal one or the conventional overt behavioural modification cue, once the problem is systematially analysed and the goals and means of treatment systematically formulated.

Of the therapies based on classical conditioning techniques, the three most frequently used are:

(1) Systematic Desensitization

(2) Flooding

(3) Aversion Therapy

Systematic Desensitization

Systematic desensitization has been used widely with phobic patients — persons with irrational and maladaptive fears. The first step is to teach the patient to become aware of deep muscle relaxation and to concentrate on relaxing when he develops tension. The patient is progressively presented with stimuli known to produce anxiety. The therapist begins with the mildest stimulus and works his way up an anxiety hierarchy to the most anxiety-provoking stimulus. When a presentation elicits no anxiety response, the therapist introduces the next stimulus in the anxiety hierarchy. This continues until the most intense stimulus elicits no anxiety. In systematic desensitization the therapist combines relaxation with an imaginary recreation of the anxiety-evoking situation until the fear situation — both real and imaginary — no longer evokes anxiety.

Flooding

This form of therapy is most frequently used with anxiety neuroses. To resolve the problem, the original painful situation must be recreated so that the individual can learn to cope with his fears. In flooding, the therapist encourages the client to confront the feared object in vivo. By creating an atmosphere devoid of the original threatening conditions, the therapist helps the patient to become undisturbed in the anxiety-provoking situation. The old threat is recreated, but under supportive circumstances. The flooding procedure assumes that the anxiety can be extinguished most effectively by repeatedly eliciting intense emotional responses without punishment or negative reinforcement. The therapist spends relatively little time finding the source of the client's anxieties. He focuses primarily on extinguishing the specific anxiety response, whatever its origins.

A development of the idea of flooding is implosive therapy. Implosion is the confronting of the feared situation in imagination and in an exaggerated and totally unrealistic form. The client is encouraged to imagine the worst possible thing that could happen and then to go beyond even this. Thus, the unrealistic aspect of the phobia is brought clearly to the client's attention and he is then encouraged to develop a more realistic perspective. This approach is the behavioural equivalent of the cognitive strategies used by Ellis in his Rational-Emotive therapy.

Aversion Therapy

Aversion therapy consists of administering an aversive stimulus to inhibit an unwanted emotional response, thereby diminishing its habit strength. Aversion is used largely in the treatment of obsessions, compulsions and addictions. Azrin and Holz (1966) give the following guidelines for aversion therapy of emotionally-based habits.

1. The stimulus should be as intense as necessary to block the pleasurable response.
2. The aversive stimulus should be delivered contemporaneously with the response.
3. The aversive stimulus should not be increased gradually, but introduced at a previously determined high intensity.
4. The frequency of administration should be as high as possible; ideally the stimulus should be given with every evocation of the response to be eliminated.
5. An alternative emotional target should be available which itself will not be punished, but which will produce the same or greater reinforcement as the target the response to which is being eliminated.
6. Aversion therapy should not be administered before seeking the possible anxiety bases of the maladaptive behaviour.

Behaviour therapy differs from psychoanalysis in its concern with actual behaviour, rather than supposed underlying causes. Behaviour therapists are agreed that the focus of their attention is on the actual behaviour of the patient. They require detailed behavioural descriptions of the patient's complaint. Having obtained a description of the presenting complaint, the behaviour therapist will then try to pinpoint events in the patient's immediate environment which are either maintaining the undesirable behaviour or are preventing the patient from learning a new mode of adjustment. Meyer and Chesser (1970) state that behaviour therapy aims to modify current symptoms and focuses attention on their behavioural manifestations in terms of observable responses. Although behaviour therapists adopt a developmental approach to the genesis of symptoms, they do not think it is always necessary to unravel their origin and subsequent development.

1.3 The Psychoanalytic Technique of Freud
In studying human behaviour, Freud maintained that it was necessary to examine it under three headings: the dynamic, the topographical and the economic. The dynamic aspect involves consideration of the id, ego and superego; the topographical stresses that conflict between these systems may occur at three possible levels, conscious, pre-conscious, unconscious; the economic aspect asserts that the resolution of any conflict occurs as the needs of the total situation demand.

The psychoanalytic technique of Freud may be said to focus especially on the client's unconscious since for him the unconscious determinants of the personality are of decisive importance. Although Freud did not discover the unconscious, he was the first to use free association and dream interpretation as methods to explore it in depth.

Free association requires the patient to express his thought freely, without concern for propriety, logical connection or reflection. This is done by being relaxed, by saying whatever comes into the mind spontaneously and, at the same time, witholding as far as possible all conscious and deliberate control of thoughts and ideas or feelings. In free association the sequences are expressive of the unconscious motivations and ideas of the patient. By reducing the degree of rational control and normal inhibition, Freud believed that the associations or fantasies of a patient would reveal patterns indicative of significant emotional problems.

He also emphasized the importance of dreams, believing they were the royal road to the unconscious. In dreams, unconscious material which might threaten sleep are translated into forms which can be tolerated without emotional disturbance. The processes of transformation of this unconscious material into symbols acceptable to the conscious ego are called the 'dream work'. These processes include the symbolism itself which involves the representation of unconscious material in commonly acceptable forms taken from everyday life without revealing their real meaning in consciousness. The latent content of dreams cannot be brought to consciousness in an absolutely undisguised form, but must be expressed in words or other symbols which can be understood by analyst and patient together and interpreted so that the emotional tensions associated in the dream are discharged and the childhood experiences proved harmless and integrated into adult life.

Free association and dream interpretation are means of bringing unconscious and unacceptable impulses and conflicts to the conscious level where they are re-experienced and analysed. The re-experience of past events refers particularly to transference, viz., the tendency of the patient to transfer onto the analyst feelings, impulses, memories and wishes associated with significant people in his past. The analyst is liked and admired (or hated and feared if the transference is negative) because the patient puts him in fantasy in the place of a significant other and behaves towards him as he behaved or wanted to behave towards that other person. Thus, within the analytic setting, the patient relives old emotions and frustrations with an intensity that often rivals that of the original experience. But the therapeutic setting is neutral and the analyst does not respond as the key figures once did. This makes it possible to re-experience the transferred memories and emotions from the past in such a manner that they lose their harmful impact. They are also subjected to rational analysis. The repressed and maladaptive experiences become part of the individual's conscious self and lose their pathological effects. The analysis of these transference responses, both positive and negative, is looked upon as the key to successful psychoanalysis.

Freudian analytic technique, accordingly, has a four-fold focus:

1. The analysis of the transference reactions, originating in the past and transferred into the analytic session and onto the analyst.
2. The interpretation or analysis of dreams reported by the patient.
3. The analysis of the material brought to awareness as a result of free association.
4. The analysis of the patient's resistance, so that the material being repressed can be brought to consciousness.

The role of the analyst is basically passive. He seeks to avoid impressing his personality on the patient, avoids solving the patient's problems for him and, above all, refrains from any kind of moralistic judgement, comment or guidance. The analyst realizes that the patient has usually applied moral censure and guidance to himself and has had them applied to him by others in futile efforts to set matters right before coming for treatment. The therapeutic task is to persuade the patient to relax the overstrained moral efforts and to seek the forces which underly the illness. Often these forces are very difficult to find, but when they are actually revealed to the patient by his own efforts under the protection and encouragement rather than the control of the analyst, and are grasped and assimilated into his normal life, tremendous changes, it is believed, will be produced. Thus the patient finds for himself that the application of moral control becomes possible for him again, and he has the immense advantage of making that discovery and putting it into action by his own efforts, instead of trying to do what somebody else dictates.

1.4 Client Centred Approach of Rogers

Rogers' approach has been called client-centred counselling or therapy. It puts emphasis on the immediate situation rather than on the client's past history as in psychoanalysis. The interpersonal relationship of client and counsellor is one of its fundamental characteristics. 'I let myself go into the immediacy of the relationship,' says Rogers (1955), 'where it is my total organism which takes over and is sensitive to the relationship, not simply my consciousness. I am not consciously responding in a playful or analytic way but simply react in an unreflective way to the other individual, my reaction being based on my total organismic sensitivity to this other person. I live the relationship on this basis.'

The client-centred approach is based on the principle that the client is the one who is responsible for his own destiny and that he has the right of choice of solution for his own problems. The counsellor imposes no restrictions on the client. Rogers (1961) states: 'I have not found it helpful to intervene in the client's experience with diagnostic explanations nor with suggestions and guidance.' Rogers contends that within each individual there are residual resources for growth which need merely to be released to enable the person to achieve maturity. Hence client-centred counselling is essentially a process of change in which emotional blocks are removed, thus allowing for maturation, growth and the assimilation of new experiences. In this process Rogers (1961) distinguishes seven stages.

First Stage

The client does not communicate about himself. He concentrates his attention on externals. He tends to see himself as having no real problem. Those problems which he does recognize, he believes to be external to him in his environment. He sees no need and has no desire to change. This type of pattern might be seen in a client who does not come voluntarily to counselling.

Second Stage

If the client feels fully received by the counsellor, a slight loosening and flow of communication occurs. The client talks more or less freely about non-self topics. He may show feelings but they seem remote, external, unappropriated by the self. Personal constructs are rigid and unrecognized contradictions are expressed.

Third Stage

There is a freer flow of expression about the self and self-related experience. Feelings are revealed as something shameful, bad, or unacceptable in many ways. There is some awareness of the rigidity of personal constructs and of contradictions in experience.

Fourth Stage

There is a freer flow of feelings, sometimes breaking through almost against the client's wishes. Mostly there is little open acceptance of them. Awareness and recognition of personal constructs takes place and an initial questioning of their validity.

Fifth Stage

Feelings are expressed as in the present. They 'bubble up' and 'seep through' and are experienced fully and immediately with a certain surprise or fright, rarely with pleasure, and they are acknowledged as belonging to the self. Personal constructs have lost much of their rigidity. Contradictions in experience are faced more clearly and an increased feeling of being responsible for oneself emerges.

Sixth Stage

Feelings flow fully and are experienced with immediacy and richness. Such physiological concomitants as tears, sighs and muscular relaxation are frequent. There is a full awareness and full acceptance of experience.

Seventh Stage

New feelings are experienced with immediacy and richness and are acknowledged as belonging to oneself and as being part of one's real self. Personal constructs are tentatively reformulated to be validated against further experience. Internal communication is clear with feelings and symbols matched and there is an experiencing of effective choice of new ways of being.

Carkhuff (1969) differs somewhat from Rogers in distinguishing five rather than seven levels in the counselling process.

Level 1. The client does not discuss personally relevant material, either because he has no opportunity to do so or because he is actively evading discussion even when it is introduced by the counsellor.

Level 2. The client *responds* with discussion to the introduction of personally relevant material by the counsellor but does so in a mechanical manner and without the demonstration of emotional feeling.

Level 3. The client *voluntarily* introduces discussion of personally relevant material but does so in a mechanical manner and without the demonstration of emotional feeling.

Level 4. The client voluntarily introduces discussion of personally relevant material with both spontaneity and emotion.

Level 5. The client engages actively and spontaneously in an inward probing to discover new feelings and experiences about himself and his world.

The emphasis in client-centred therapy, then, is on being a person. This is a dynamic, not a static process. Whereas psychoanalysis emphasizes the unconscious and the technical skills of the analyst, and behaviour therapy emphasizes the impact of carefully programmed conditioning, contemporary client-centred counselling focuses on consciousness and, while involving specific counselling or therapeutic skills, it considers certain 'core conditions' as of even greater importance for a successful therapeutic outcome. These 'core conditions' will be discussed in chapter 3.

2

Counselling: *Techniques and Goals*

2.1 Client-Centred Counselling Techniques

Rogers (1951), Carkhuff (1972) and Patterson (1974) believe that certain techniques can be adopted by client-centred therapy which will assist the counsellor to apply or implement the appropriate core counselling conditions. The most frequently used techniques are the following:

(1) Structuring
(2) Listening
(3) Silence
(4) Responding
(5) Reflection
(6) Questioning
(7) Interpretation

(1) Structuring

Structuring is the orientation of the client to his own role and to the role of the counsellor in their relationship. If he enters the relationship by taking the responsibility for presenting himself and his problems and concerns, it is not necessary for the counsellor to engage in formal structuring. Formal structuring is necessary, according to Patterson (1974), only when (a) the client has no idea about what either the counsellor or himself is expected to do and (b) the client has a misconception of what the counsellor does or what he (the client) is expected to do. According to Eisenberg and Delaney (1976), structuring is the most reasonable way to increase the reluctant client's readiness for the counselling experience. This means that the counsellor must clearly inform the client as to the reasons and goals for the session and must present the data related to the problem situation in descriptive rather than inferential or abstract terms. More frequently the client will take responsibility for presenting himself and his problems and concerns. To engage in structuring in this situation would only disrupt the process.

Various structuring techniques can be used during the course of counselling.

1. When a client digresses and discusses people and topics not related to the problem area, the counsellor may say, e.g., 'I'd like to get back to your problem with your mother.'
or
'How does this relate to the problem with your mother?'
or
'You said earlier that your mother is always picking on you.'

2. When an area has been covered to the counsellor's satisfaction, it is possible to change to another topic by making transition statements. 'You have told me about your relationship with your mother, tell me now how you get on with your father.'
or
'I would like to know something about the rest of your family.'

3. When a student comes in emotionally upset and says that he doesn't know why he is disturbed, the counsellor might start with 'Tell me about today'.

(2) Listening

'Real communication occurs,' states Rogers (1961), 'when we listen with understanding.' He goes on to say that 'listening is the most effective agent we know for altering the basic personality structure of an individual and improving his relationships and his communication with others.'

If the counsellor is to understand the client, he must allow the client to present himself. Only the client can tell the counsellor how he feels, what he thinks, how he sees himself and his world. Only by listening to the client can the counsellor enter his world and see things as he does. However, the counsellor must think *with* the client. There are four ways of thinking with, namely:

1. Restating what the client said to let him know that he was understood.
Client: No matter how hard I try I can't seem to get a grasp of that subject.
Counsellor: I can see that you find it difficult to understand that subject.

2. Pausing, nodding, waiting for further information.
Client: I just feel that people pick on me ... today was the last straw ...
Counsellor: (Pauses and waits for the client to give more information. Positive non-verbal encouragement is important here.)

3. Asking for more information but *not* directing the conversation.

Client: I'm down in the dumps.
Counsellor: Would you like to tell me more about it?

4. Guiding the client in examining his own feelings and finding his own answers.

Client: My dad told me the other night that I looked relaxed. How would he know? I am doing honours maths and I really hate it but I need honours for college. I want to do Science and then get into pre-med.
Counsellor: Your dad told you that you looked relaxed — how do you feel?
Client: Awful . . . all tensed up really . . . . .
Counsellor: What would help you feel better . . . ?

Hence thinking with the client involves allowing him the opportunity to present himself with complete freedom and without the constraint of another's frame of reference. This involves the counsellor avoiding *not* (a) thinking for (b) thinking about and (c) thinking against the client.

There are four main ways of *thinking for*.

1. Interrupting the client, putting words into his mouth.

Client: Mr O'Brien has it in for me . . . we haven't . . . .
Counsellor: I'm sure he hasn't. He probably has problems of his own.

2. Directing the conversation.

Client: All the other girls do it, sleep with their boyfriends, I mean . . . . I just feel scared about doing it . . . . .
Counsellor: How do you think your parents would react if they thought that you'd slept with your boyfriend?

3. Giving advice prematurely.

Client: Nothing's been right since my husband died two years ago. I literally slave for these children. Up early to get to work. Back in the evening to get the meals . . . You'd think those kids would have more gratitude and help me a little. But the older they get, the more selfish they get.

Counsellor: Looks like you'll have to get wise. Take away some of their privileges or something — just make them do things for themselves instead of leaving it all up to yourself.

4. Restating what the client has said, but changing its emphasis or implications.

Client: I cringe every time people ask me about my education. As soon as I say 'Leaving Cert' I see their minds turn off. I feel that I am as educated as any college graduate. I read quite a bit.
Counsellor: You feel that a college education is unnecessary, particularly if you do a lot of reading.

The counsellor must really be interested in what the client says, not just waiting for his chance to speak, not just *thinking about* what he is going to say to him. There are three ways of doing this.

1. Giving 'pat' answers of the 'popular psychology' type.

Client: The trouble with the rest of the gang is that they put me under a lot of pressure . . . to drink, I mean.
Counsellor: Well, it is a very well known fact that 'group pressure' plays a big role in influencing young people in starting to experiment with drink.

2. Analysing the participant's motivation.

Client: I really can't think about doing anything else with my life except being a teacher, although I'm not sure I'd really like to be one!
Counsellor: Perhaps you think you want to be a teacher because both your parents are in the teaching profession?

3. Giving theoretical pronouncements of the 'everyone feels that way' type.

Client: I feel so bad, I just can't seem to get down to work and the exams are around the corner, I don't think I can cope.
Counsellor: Most people feel this way before exams. It's only natural that you feel badly. But don't worry . . .

Thinking against can take the following forms.

1. Arguing or disagreeing.

   Client: All my friends think that you shouldn't experiment with drugs . . . I think that they are just afraid . . . I think that everyone should experiment to see what they are like . . . Why not?
   Counsellor: I do not think so. I think that you are wrong to think that everyone should do this — the danger of becoming hooked . . .

2. Implying or stating that 'you shouldn't feel that way'.

   Client: I feel so depressed and bored with school.
   Counsellor: How could you be bored with school? Think of all the exciting things e.g. sports/art that you can do, apart from having plenty of exercises to fill in your time.

3. Implying or stating a threat to the client.

   Client: If he gets at me once more in class, I'm going to really let him have a few once the teacher is gone.
   Counsellor: If you do that, you are liable to be expelled . . .

4. Being defensive — justifying oneself.

   Client: I really don't know what to do . . . you're no help at all . . .
   Counsellor: Well, how can I help you if you refuse to be honest . . .

Real listening is not a passive but an active process. Two important dimensions of listening are attention and time. The counsellor must give his complete attention and give it in such a manner that the client is aware that this is happening. He recognises that the counsellor is attending to him through the way he looks at him and he is certain of this attention when there is eye contact between them. The counsellor, therefore, should look at the client, particularly at his face and usually at his eyes.

Along with eye-contact, the body posture of the counsellor is another critical element in attending physically. This has two functions: (1) as a sign to the client that the counsellor is working with him and (2) it helps the counsellor to listen actively. His physically attentive posture helps his psychological attending. When the counsellor inclines his body towards the client he thereby signals his attention to the client. When standing, he achieves this by closing the physical distance between himself and the client. Egan (1975) indicates five ways for physical attending:

1. Face the other person squarely.
2. Adopt an open posture.
3. Lean toward the other.
4. Keep good eye contact.
5. Try to be 'at home' or relatively relaxed in this position.

Real listening has to be learnt. Frieda Fromm-Reichman (1950) writes:'To be able to listen to another person in this other person's own right, without reacting along the lines of one's own problems or experiences, of which one may be reminded, perhaps in a disturbing way, is an act of interpersonal exchange which few people are able to practise without special training.'

(3) Silence

Two types of silence can be distinguished: (a) the silence of active listening and (b) the silence of non-participation. Some clients may fail to return to counselling because they are uncertain whether the therapist was really listening to them, was interested in them, understood them or accepted them. Their revelation of socially undesirable thoughts or behaviour may prompt them to feel not accepted, not understood, or rejected. It is desirable, therefore, that the counsellor does not remain silent, but responds, conveying his understanding or acceptance of them. No response may be seen by the client as rejection or an indication that he is being irrelevant. Silence is useful in extinguishing irrelevant talk but one must be careful because it can extinguish all talking.

(4) Responding

Counselling is not a conventional social conversation and for the counsellor to adopt such an approach initially is misleading. Eldred et al. (1954) found that having to shift from conventional pleasantries to the work of therapy did not help the therapeutic process. When the counsellor feels that the client is engaging in irrelevant talk, he withholds response. This lack of response extinguishes the client's irrelevant talk.

On the other hand when the client is anxious and finds it hard to talk, the counsellor can encourage the client by responses such as: 'I know that you are concerned about these problems. Relax and just tell me in your own time.'

In this way, the counsellor conveys to the client that his feelings are accepted. Responsiveness on the part of the counsellor facilitates deeper exploration and greater self-revelation by the client. A particular difficulty arises when the client is unwilling or unable to talk. Wolberg (1967) suggests a number of techniques to overcome this client silence.

a: Say 'mm-hmm' or 'Yes' or 'I see' and wait a moment.
b: Repeat the last word or last few words.
c: Repeat the last sentence or recast it as a question.
d: Say 'and' or 'but' with a questioning emphasis as if something else is to follow.
e: 'You find it difficult to talk.'
f: 'I wonder why you are silent.'
g: 'Perhaps you do not know what to say?'
h: 'Perhaps you are upset.'
i: A direct attack on the resistance — 'Perhaps you are afraid to say what is on your mind.'

Responding also involves communicating the counsellor's understanding of what the client is saying to him. This can be accomplished by the use of such phrases as

a: Let me be sure I understand . . .
b: Am I right in saying that this is how you see it?
c: What I hear you saying is . . .
d: I'm confused about this last point. Can you clarify it?

The counsellor by his responsiveness or lack of responsiveness influences the content and the manner of the client's communication. He selects from the client's productions those which he feels are most relevant and he responds to them, while ignoring others.

(5) Reflection

The client's verbalizations, especially when he is disturbed, are not always clear and obvious. They may be confused, jumbled, hesitant, incomplete, disordered or fragmentary. In his reflection responses, the counsellor attempts to put together what the client is saying or trying to say, to put into words vague ideas or feelings that are implicit or explicit. What is confused to the client may not be clear to the therapist either, so that reflection responses are not always easy to formulate and the therapist may often be unsure of their accuracy.

Reflection may be viewed under three headings:

(1) Simple Reflection.
(2) Content Reflection.
(3) Feeling Reflection.

In *simple reflection*, the counsellor echoes the last few words which the client said before pausing. Alternatively, he may rephrase the last few words expressing the same meaning as the client. The reflection can be literal or rephrased.

Content reflection is a short, simple restatement of the essence of what the client has actually said. Content reflection condenses and crystallises the information in a fresh way. Telschow (1950) found that restatement of content by the counsellor is, therapeutically, somewhat more effective than simple acceptance of feeling.

Often the content reflection may not communicate the real underlying meaning. *Feeling reflection* focuses on this, picking out from the whole body of statements made by the client a few words or phrases that appear to carry suppressed emotion.

Client: I don't think I could do it. I'd only fail. I . . . well − I've never been able to get grades like that before and I'm sure I couldn't now.
Counsellor: (Content reflection) Your past records convince you it's not possible now.
(Feeling reflection) You're feeling a bit afraid even to try.

Which of these reflection responses is appropriate to use depends on the particular situation. Hence, when a client says 'No, I won't! I'm not going to tell you any of my business. I didn't ask to see you. I was sent! You're not getting anything out of me', the counsellor may use a feeling reflection response like 'You are angry at being sent here'. If, on the other hand, a client says 'Well, O.K., the problem is at home. But what difference does it make talking to you? You wouldn't understand. You just don't know what it's like there day after day', the counsellor may use the content reflection response: ' So the problem is at home'.

(6) Questioning

One of the basic distinctions is that between the open and closed question. The openness of a question is a matter of degree. Questions vary from those which restrict the client's response completely to those which do so minimally, e.g. 'Do you feel angry?' to 'How do you feel?'

According to Lindzey (1954) an open question gives the client little or no guidance as to the form or content of his answer. It allows him to choose the level and scope of his answer to suit himself. Open questions are usually very appropriate at the beginning of a session. The open question solicits the client's views, opinions, thoughts and feelings. It establishes rapport.

A closed question, on the other hand, limits the client's answer. It specifies a series of options, sometimes only two, from which the client is to choose.

Closed Question	*Types of Answers*
(1) Is your name Joan Murphy?	(1) Yes/No.
(2) Do you get up at 8 a.m., before 8 a.m. or after 8 a.m.?	(2) One of three.

A closed question asks the client to recognize a fact, an idea or a behaviour. It can be valuable if used in an appropriate place e.g. to clarify a point — 'Are you afraid of your mother?' However it does not give the client much opportunity to express himself. If used too frequently, the encounter turns into a series of often superfluous closed questions and largely uninformative 'yes' or 'no' answers. The client does not take the initiative and is discouraged from engaging in the process of exploration.

Three types of questions may be used to encourage client exploration, (1) the problem question, (2) the probe question and (3) the link question.

(1) *The Problem Question*
'What would you do if your wife left you?'
This kind of question is useful in getting the client thinking and talking. It can aid the client in the process of decision-making.

(2) *The Probe Question*
'Better in what way?'
This type of question is used as a follow-up. It could be used to clarify a point or to invite the client to be more precise or to stimulate him to think through an issue for himself.

(3) *The Link Question*
'Speaking of Rachel, tell me about the other members of the family.'

These questions are useful to lead the conversation back to the subject or on to a new subject. At the same time they maintain the flow of conversation and its continuity.

In conclusion, it can be stated that questions add to the directionality of the session and place legitimate demands for concreteness on the client.

(7) Interpretation

Rogers (1962) defines interpretation as ' the counsellor's understanding of what is vaguely known to the client and the ability to voice meanings in the client's experience of which he is scarcely aware.' However, the counsellor should direct his interpretations at material that is just below the surface or outside of the client's conscious awareness. Speisman (1959) confirmed that interpretations dealing with matters remote from conscious awareness evoke resistance.

Unlike other interventions, interpretation, according to Weiner (1975), deals with unconscious material rather than with manifest productions. It seeks to explain rather than describe the client's behaviour. It consists of inferences, probabilities and alternative hypotheses rather than observations, facts and certainties.

Garduk and Haggard (1972) identified the following specific effects of interpretation.

(1) Longer reaction times on the part of the client.
(2) Less verbal activity and more silence in response to interpretation.
(3) More emotion.
(4) Defensive associations.
(5) More indications of understanding, 'Yes, I can understand that', and insight, 'I wouldn't have thought of that but I recognize it now.'

It is important to note that interpretation does not end with a dramatic and conclusive statement delivered by the counsellor. 'So it appears that being alone makes you anxious, as if you're afraid something bad might happen in that kind of situation.' Interpretation serves not only to summarise what has previously been said but also to stimulate *new* lines of inquiry. The client explores the implications of the interpretation and takes the next step on his own Tarachow (1963) states that interpretations involve a sense of loss since the person has to give up a set way of psychic functioning.

In interpretation, the counsellor transcends the client's verbalisation and puts in something of his own. The line between reflection and interpretation is a fine one. What is reflection to a highly sensitive counsellor may appear to be interpretation to one who is less sensitive to the implication of the client's words. Rogers (1962) speaks of interpretation thus: 'When the client's world is clear to the counsellor and he can move about in it freely, then he can communicate his understanding of what is vaguely known to the client and can also voice meanings in the client's experience of which the client is scarcely aware.' Martin (1972) writes: ' The coun-

sellor's task is to hear what is implicit in the client's current experiencing
– what the client is trying to say and can't quite say.' According to
Porter (1959) the difference between reflection and interpretation is not
in the words used but in the reasons for saying them. When the counsellor
restates what the client has expressed and when his intention is to ascertain from him whether or not his restatement is an accurate expression
of the client's meaning, that is a reflection. When, on the other hand,
the purpose of the counsellor is to communicate the real underlying
meaning of the client's expression, not the apparent meaning communicated by him, that is interpretation.

2.2 The Goals of Counselling
The goals of counselling are numerous. According to Eisenberg and Delaney
(1976), it aims to help individuals to achieve such objectives as the following:

—understanding self,
—making important personal decisions,
—setting personal goals that are achievable and growth-enhancing,
—developing plans in the present to bring about possible and desired
    futures,
—developing effective solutions to personal and interpersonal problems,
—changing ineffective behaviour to more effective behaviour,
—coping with difficult environmental and life-space circumstances,
—gaining control over negative and self- defeating emotions such as
    debilitating anxiety, guilt, self-pity, loneliness, alienation, hopeless-
    ness and basic insecurity,
—acquiring and learning to use effective interpersonal transaction skills,
—acquiring a sense of basic liking and respect for self and a sense of
    optimism about one's ability to satisfy one's basic needs.

In this study the emphasis is placed on the 'healing help' by which the
counsellor enables the client to become a 'whole' person. The life of a
whole person is made up of actions integrating fully his emotional,
intellectual and physical resources in such a way that these actions lead to
even greater self-definition.

This view resembles that of Rogers who sees counselling as gradually
allowing the client to move (1) away from undue dependence upon others,
(2) towards self-direction and free responsible choosing, (3) towards openness to life and experience, (4) towards trust of self and others, and
(5) towards a greater creativeness in thought, word and action. Undue
dependence upon others is revealed in the need to hide behind a mask in

order to be accepted. It is shown in an excessive submission to behaviour standards imposed by parents and parent substitutes. It is revealed in a constant endeavour to live up to the expectations of others, to please others, to bow to their standards, and to yield to their pressures for conformity.

A second main objective in the Rogerian tradition is achievement of self-direction and free responsible choice. By and within the counselling process, the extension of personal freedom and the activity of authentic personal choice remains a real goal. As therapy proceeds, the client finds that he is daring to become himself. He realizes that he can choose to hide behind a facade or take the risks involved in being himself. He becomes aware that he is a free agent who has the power to destroy another or himself and the power to enhance himself and others. This does not solve problems. It opens up a new way of living in which there is more height and depth in the experiencing of his feelings and a greater range of awareness of where he wants to go.

Thus freedom of choice and the reality of openness to experience are closely allied. Effective counselling ensures that a person moves towards living in an open, friendly relationship with his own experience. This does not occur easily. Often, as the client experiences some new facet of himself, he rejects and denies it initially. Only gradually does he learn that experiencing is a friendly resource, not a terrifying enemy. This greater openness to inner experience is associated with a similar openness to all aspects of external reality. Rogers (1971) has summed up the goals of counselling and therapy well when he described clients as 'people who move towards being persons who accept and even enjoy their own feelings, who value and trust the deeper layers of their nature, who find strength in their own uniqueness and who live by values they experience. This learning, this movement, enables them to live as more individuated, more creative and more responsible persons.'

3

Core Conditions: *Theory and Research*

3.1 Core Conditions: Theory
In chapters 1 and 2 the basic nature, main approaches, techniques and goals of client-centred counselling have been discussed. There is, however, a number of core conditions without which such counselling is considered to be largely ineffecitve. In this chapter we consider these conditions of empathy, congruence, level of regard and unconditionality and the research findings concerning them.

3.2 Empathy
In the moment to moment encounter of counselling, the ability of the counsellor to obtain an accurate and sensitive understanding of the experiences and feelings of the client and the significance which these have for the client is of paramount importance. This accurate and sensitive understanding is termed 'empathy'.

Rogers (1951) defined empathy as the ability to assume the internal frame of reference of the client, to perceive the client as he is seen by himself, to lay aside all perceptions from an external frame of reference while doing so and to communicate something of this understanding. The counsellor tries to feel his way about the internal world of thought and feeling of the other in order to come as close to him as possible, to understand him as much as possible.

Barrett-Lennard (1962) sees empathic understanding as an active process of desiring to know the present and changing awareness of another person, of reaching out to receive his communication and meaning, and of translating his words and signs into experienced meaning that matches those aspects of his awareness that are most important to him at the moment. It is an experiencing of the consciousness behind another's outward communication, but with the continuous awareness that this consciousness is originating and proceeding in the other.

From these definitions, it would appear that there is a consensus that the empathic counsellor explores with the client his internal world of thought and feeling so that the client may come closer to his own world, his own self. The empathic counsellor so cares for the client that he is willing to abandon, temporarily, his own interests in order to think, act, and feel as if the life of the other were his very own. In this way, the client senses that the counsellor really cares about him because the counsellor has tried so hard to understand.

The understanding of the client requires not only an understanding of his words, but also of his meanings, including those meanings not yet fully conceptualized into awareness. According to Glendlin (1962), empathic understanding points sensitively to the felt meaning which the client is experiencing in a particular moment in order to help him focus on that meaning and to carry it further to its full and uninhibited experiencing. This is in close agreement with Truax (1967) who says that empathic understanding occurs when the counsellor interprets correctly all the client's present acknowledged feelings. The counsellor also tries to uncover the most deeply shrouded of the client's feeling areas, voicing meanings in the client's experience of which the client is scarcely aware. He becomes alive to feelings and experiences that are only hinted at by the client and does so with sensitivity and accuracy. He conveys this to the client by way of direct information or suggestion or whatever means his growing understanding of the client would indicate. Through this, the client broadens his understanding of himself and is able to allow into his awareness more of the actual experiencing taking place at what Powell (1969) refers to as 'gut' level. To be understood in this deep, thorough and accepting sense is a very confirmatory experience. It gives both clarity and affirmation to the growing confidence in his self-concept which the client is experiencing. Hence, the experience of being understood is itself a very powerful growth influence.

Although an accurate empathic understanding is very helpful, the *intent to understand* is itself of value. When the client realises that the counsellor is trying to understand his confused and uncertain statements, it encourages him to communicate more of himself and helps him to recognise that the counsellor perceives his feelings and meanings as worth understanding and that he, therefore, is worthwhile.

In empathic understanding, the counsellor tries to get within and to *live* the attitudes expressed by the client instead of observing them, to catch every nuance of their changing nature, in a word, to absorb himself completely in the attitudes of the other. It involves following the advice given by the father to his daughter in Harper Lee's novel *To Kill a Mockingbird*: 'You never really understand a person until you consider a thing from his point of view, until you climb into his skin and walk around in it.' Freud (1921) expressed the same idea when he described empathy as the mechanism by which we are enabled to adapt our attitudes towards another's mental life.

In attempting to empathise in this manner, there is simply no room for any other type of counsellor activity. If he is attempting to live the attitudes of the other, he cannot be diagnosing them. Because he is another, and not the client, the understanding is not spontaneous and so must be acquired. This can only happen through the most intense, continuous and active attention to the feelings of the other to the exclusion of any other type of attention. Heine (1950) and Fielder (1950) emphasized this complete participation in the client's communication as the most characteristic feature of the ideal counselling relationship.

In their discussion of the perceptive dimension in counselling, Truax and Mitchell (1971) state that:

'Intense focusing on the other person is central to the perceptive dimension of empathic understanding, since it allows us to note not merely verbal but subtle non-verbal communications — the minute facial, postural and gestural clues that may contradict or confirm the meaning of another person's verbal communications. This intense focusing of the other person also tends to ensure that errors in either our perception or our communication of understanding will be quickly detected by us. We will be able to sense when our communications do not fit exactly and, sometimes in mid-sentence, we can shift to correct for errors of language or content. In short, our intense and intimate focusing on the other person makes possible the moment to moment rapport necessary for accurate empathic understanding.'

Many of the cues used for deciding what is true, false, or meaningful derive from our own experience. We can often recognise from our awareness of ourselves the outward signs that relate to inner feelings and experiences. Basically, of course, we rely upon moment by moment changes in the other person as a sign of what is significant. A blush, a stammer, a flood of words, a change in breathing, a tensing of posture, may be much more important than what the other person, at that moment, is saying in words.

Tone also gives useful clues to the client's feeling. It includes level of voice, pitch and voice quality. In sadness and melancholy the voice is low, faint and broken; anger can lead to an increase in volume and a raising of pitch, though when controlled it merely aquires a cutting sharpness of tone. The voice of fear is high and gasping and may issue at times in shrill hysteria. The cherishing, loving tone is warming, welcoming and accepting.

The client can also give the counsellor many clues to his experience by his physical behaviour. When verbal clues to the client's experience are confusing the counsellor, he can refer to the evidence of the client's non-verbal behaviour. A favourite technique of Frieda Fromm-Reichman, for example, was to imitate a client's posture herself in order to obtain some feeling for what he was experiencing. Deutsh (1951) suggests that feelings and attitudes are closely related to characteristic postures and gestures. For example, a depressed person speaks lifelessly and 'hangs' his head forward; a tense person stands rigidly and is tense in his verbal and physical behaviour; a confident person tends to carry himself erectly.

The 'distance' between individuals is an important variable in inter-personal situations. It may also have a significant influence on a client's perception of the situation. Sommer (1959) and Haase and Di Mattia (1970) suggested that an arrangement in which the space between the chairs is partially intersected by the desk may have the advantage of being open enough to allow interaction, while still offering protection under circumstances which may evoke feelings of uncertainty or anxiety in a client. According to Little (1965), 'personal space' designates the area immediately surrounding an individual in which the majority of his inter-action with others takes place. Intrusion into this space may cause severe discomfort.

Carkhuff (1969) distinguishes between *interchangeable* empathy res-ponses and *additive* empathy responses. Interchangeable responses are those which capture accurately and reflect back to a client the essential part of his or her message. While they do not add meaning to the client's stated message, neither do they subtract any significant data from the mess-age. Thus they are considered interchangeable. By contrast, additive res-ponses add significantly to the feeling and meaning of the expressions of the client in such a way as to express accurately feeling levels beyond what the client was able to express. The counsellor responds with accuracy to all of the client's deeper as well as surface feelings. Because the additive levels go beyond the client's stated message, the components which are added or inferred are hypothesized from what the client has said. This being so, the additive parts must be stated tentatively, rather than with certainty. In each type of response, the counsellor highlights or emphasizes the feel-ing aspect of the client's message. In additive empathy responses, the coun-sellor must be careful to distinguish between what he heard (actually received in transmission) and what he inferred (hypothesized on the basis of the information offered).

The concept of empathy should be distinguished from such concepts as identification, projection and sympathy. Empathy can be distinguished from identification in that the latter involves the emotions more deeply and occurs less frequently. Healy, Bronner and Bowers (1930) defined identification as ' the unconscious moulding of one's own ego after the fashion of one who has been taken as a model'. In empathy, however, there is no implication that one would want unconsciously to be like the other person, nor does empathy necessarily imply any emotional tie with the other. Roger (1949) makes this distinction when he says of empathy that 'the experiencing with the client, the living of his attitudes, is not in terms of an emotional involvement on the counsellor's part'.

Projection, an antithetical process to empathy, involves the attribution of one's own wishes, attitudes and behaviour to someone other than one's own self. The shared experience which is empathy is based to a certain extent on remembered corresponding affective states of one's own. When we observe a person's life at any one point, we project tentatively onto him the feelings we once felt under similar circumstances, and then test this projection by further observation. Through awareness of one's affective response to another and his response to it, one gains some comprehension of the emotional state of the other. Predictions based on projection, therefore, may be accurate but one runs the risk of distorting reality by impressing onto others one's own meanings. In empathy, on the other hand, every effort is made to understand the other from the other's point of view.

Empathy is not a synonym for sympathy. Koestler (1949) distinguishes between the two concepts when he states that empathy refers to the experience of partial identity between the subject's mental processes and those of another, with the resulting insight into the other's mental state. Empathy, he claims, becomes sympathy when to this mental resonance is added the desire to help. Mead, more than ten years previously in 1934, had said:

'Sympathy springs from the same capacity [as empathy] to take the role of the other person with whom one is socially implicated. Sympathy always implies that one stimulates oneself to the assistance and consideration of another by taking, to some degree, the attitude of the other person whom one is willing to assist.'

Although accepting Koestler's and Mead's definitions of sympathy as a desire to help, it would appear that a clearer distinction can be made between these two characteristics. Empathy always involves understanding whereas sympathy need not. This contradicts Koestler's view that empathy becomes sympathy since the basic component of understanding may be lacking from sympathy. It also calls into question Shertzer and Shelly's

(1974) view that sympathy involves feeling completely what the other person feels.

Sympathy involves sharing common feelings, interests or loyalties. Empathy is different from sympathy because it does not contain the element of condolence, agreement or pity essential for sympathy. Clifford Shaw, in his book *The Jack Roller*, made this distinction when discussing his technique in dealing with problem boys:

> 'The first step in the course of treatment is the approach to the boy, not by sympathy, but by empathy. Through his life-history his counsellor is enabled to see his life as the boy conceived it rather than as an adult might imagine it. Empathy means entering into the experience of another person by the human and democratic method of sharing experiences. In this and other ways rapport is established.'

3.3 Congruence

Within the counselling relationship, the personal impact of the counsellor is highly important. What he does, what he feels, the attitudes he holds as a person, all influence the quality and depth of the relationship.

Congruence is the ability of the counsellor to bring his total personality to bear on his relationship with the client. This means that the counsellor is his true self. Congruence excludes any pretence of acting or of being what one is not; it implies honesty, candour, self-awareness and self-acceptance on the part of the counsellor and precludes any element of role playing. Moustakas (1974) emphasizes that the more integrated the counsellor is in himself, the more effective he will be: 'I saw that I must stop playing the role of the professional therapist,' he wrote, 'and allow my potentials, talents and skills, my total experience as a human being to blend naturally into the relationship.'

Halmos (1966) reinforces this idea when he states that the counsellor not merely employs a certain technique, knowledge or skill to achieve his objectives but that the quality of his entire personality pervades the process and influences its outcome.

Because of this, the counselling relationship is affected by all that makes the counsellor what he is, and this includes his philosophy of life and his values. Rogers (1961) believes that the counsellor can help others only to the extent that he himself has grown as a person. 'The degree,' he wrote, 'to which I can create relationships which facilitate the growth of others as separate persons is a measure of the growth I have achieved in myself.' It is notable that these writers emphasize the personal rather than the professional impact of the counsellor in the relationship.

Congruence is often equated with genuineness. Truax and Carkhuff (1967) define genuineness as 'that state of the counsellor in which his verbal and non-verbal behaviour correspond with his experiencing'. Rogers (1967) agrees and holds that being real or congruent involves the difficult task of being acquainted with the flow of experiencing going on within oneself, a flow marked especially by complexity and continuous change.

While it is evident that congruence is an important part of the counselling relationship, we have to ask if limits exist. Rogers (1967), for example, says: 'If I sense that I am feeling bored by my contacts with this client, I think I owe it to him and to our relationship to share this feeling with him.' Carkhuff (1969), like Rogers, endorses the practice of some counsellors who bring their feelings out openly because then the client has the opportunity to deal with them.

Both Rogers and Carkhuff would appear to distort somewhat the concept of genuineness. Patterson (1969) has made two major points in this respect. Firstly, genuineness does not mean total disclosure since some expressions of counsellor feelings may be unhelpful or damaging to the client, for example, the manifestation of hostility towards him. Secondly, it does signify, however, that those aspects of himself that the counsellor reveals must be relevant and appropriate. Patterson would appear to reflect more precisely the counselling relationship since he displays a sensitivity which appears to be lacking in the other two approaches. Furthermore, if counselling is viewed as a contract between counsellor and client for the purpose of the emotional healing and development of the latter, surely this excludes the counsellor from using the encounter to work out his own conflicts. Moreover, the luxury of such self-disclosure on the part of the counsellor is at variance with the other-centredness which is the essence of counselling.

It may be argued that the greater the self-disclosure of the counsellor, the greater the self-disclosure of the client. Jourard (1959), for example, measured self-disclosure within a group of nine female nursing college faculty members and found that the amount disclosed to a given colleague correlated highly with the amount of disclosure received. Jourard and Landsman (1960) obtained similar results with a group of nine male graduate students. Further evidence for the reciprocity effect was obtained by Jourard and Richman (1963) who correlated subjects' reports of disclosure output and input in relationships with mother, father, best male friend, and best female friend.

One criticism of these studies is that the subject may be merely imitating the response of the experimenter rather than engaging in a reciprocation process. On the other hand, it may be held that self-disclosure by the client is what counselling seeks to achieve, and it does not matter whether the psychodynamic process be reciprocation or imitation. It is felt, however, that the nature of the process may indeed be crucial since imitative self-disclosure may lack the voluntary nature that counselling implies.

Yet it is the task of the counsellor to seek information about the client's private self. Vondracek (1969) reported greater amounts of disclosure when the interviewer used a probing technique rather than a self-revelatory approach. Tuckman (1966) concurs with this when he states that 'probing' is more effective than self-revelation in eliciting highly intimate information. Indeed, Vondracek and Vondracek (1971) and Polansky (1967), on the basis of their researches, have maintained that disclosure to certain clients could have an adverse effect on the course of counselling. Hood and Back (1971) point out that subjects expect to disclose in the experimental situation and that the opportunity to do so is a major reason for their coming to the experiment. These same authors also found that volunteers disclose more than non-volunteers. Since a necessary prerequisite of counselling is its voluntary nature, Hood and Back's findings indicate that the client comes to the counselling situation with a willingness to disclose which is independent of the level of the counsellor's self-disclosure. From these studies we may conclude that any benefits derived from self-disclosure by counsellors as a counselling technique are minimal and that probing is a better method of eliciting self-disclosure from clients.

Congruence should guard against the counsellor using the relationship to resolve his own conflicts. Freud used the term countertransference to signify those attitudes, impulses and feelings emerging in the counsellor which are alien to the analyst's function of understanding, accepting, and relating to his client. Freud believed that unresolved neurotic problems in the therapist or counsellor could or would impede the therapeutic relationship. Congruence, on the other hand, implies that the counsellor is aware of these aspects of his person and controls them consciously in the counselling situation. Therefore, in contrast to countertransference, congruence signifies that the counsellor is fully cognisant of his own relevant emotions. He is aware of them, accepts them and is able to live them positively and constructively in the relationship with his clients. Rogers believed that unless the counsellor is able to listen acceptingly to what is going on within himself, his clients will find it difficult to trust him sufficiently to explore with him their own inner experience. If, however, this ability to listen acceptingly is clearly present in the counsellor, self-exploration, self-disclosure and self-acceptance by the client are greatly facilitated.

3.4 Level of Regard

Rogers (1951) emphasized the importance of 'unconditional positive regard' in counselling. He equated it with deep and genuine caring by the counsellor for the client as a person who has many constructive potentialities. Caring is a core condition for healing. Aylwin (1979) states: 'Care cherishes, it honours the integrity of the other.' The counsellor listens, allowing the client to say what he wants to say. In expressing his anger, his sense of guilt, fear, or injustice, the client works through to an acceptance that brings healing. In this atmosphere of care, there can be neither guilt for shortcomings nor embarrassment for virtues. Within it, wounds are healed, new learning and insight acquired.

Barrett-Lennard (1959) distinguished two components of what he calls 'level of regard' and 'unconditionality'. He defined level of regard as 'the over-all level of one person's affective response to another. It is the composite "loadings" of all the distinguishable feeling reaction of one person to another.' Positive feelings include respect, liking, appreciation and affection. Negative feelings include dislike, impatience and contempt.

Level of regard thus deals with the quality of the relationship which exists between the counsellor and client. Butler (1952) revived Dewey's term 'appraising' to illustrate this concept. Appraising implies an ongoing process of comparison and selection in which values are assigned to the various aspects of the person thus evaluated. In theory, a counsellor ought not to feel dislike for, or disapproval of, a client. But counsellors are human and are subject to likes and dislikes. It is erroneous to suggest that the feelings of the counsellor do not matter because he is prohibited from allowing these feelings to enter the situation. Despite his best efforts, these feelings are betrayed by tone, gesture and facial expression. For Snyder (1946), when the counsellor feels an inability to accept the client, or has a sense of disapproval of him, the basic warmth towards the client is weakened. He is convinced that it would be better for the counsellor not to treat the client than to attempt to cover up. Snyder, however, does not give any description of this critical level of regard nor does he indicate how it could be assessed in any objective manner.

Laing (1967) observes that ' when two persons are in a relationship, the behaviour of each towards the other is mediated by the experience of each of the other, and the experience of each is mediated by the behaviour of each'. This raises the question of the basis on which liking and disliking is established in the counselling relationship. It can be maintained that in any social or interpersonal relationship, there is an almost automatic tendency for liking to breed liking and disliking to breed disliking. Taguiri (1958) and Taguiri, Blake and Brumer (1953) showed that subjects in an experimental situation think that both their likes and dislikes are reciprocated. Taguiri (1958) also found that liking is indeed symmetrical at a level well above chance. Disliking, though it may be so perceived, is not in fact symmetrical more often than chance would permit. Within the counselling relationship, then, this would seem to imply that if the counsellor likes the client, the client in turn will like the counsellor. If the counsellor dislikes the client, it does not necessarily follow that the client will dislike him. Perhaps, then, Snyder's (1946) conclusion that a counsellor who dislikes his client should not counsel him, needs considerable qualification.

Backman and Secord (1959) verified the hypothesis that 'other things being equal, the probability of person A being attracted to person B will be higher if B is perceived by A as liking A'. In a group situation, Kelly and Shapiro (1954) and Dittes and Kelly (1956) found that subjects who became aware of positive ratings of themselves by fellow group members differed significantly in their desire to remain in the group from those made aware of negative ratings. Similarly, Dittes (1959), who permitted subjects to see fictitious ratings of themselves by others, found that the more accepted members were significantly more attracted to the group as a group than were the less accepted members. In the counselling situation, this raises the question whether the counsellor should communicate felt liking for the client early in the relationship. In cases of substantial client insecurity this issue is important. Walster's (1965) research has shown that the greater a person's insecurity and self-doubt, the more he will need the counsellor to like him.

Level of regard, then, is a vital counselling condition for a seriously maladjusted client. Yet it is of relative rather than absolute importance in the counselling relationship. If it falls below the critical level, it may hinder the therapeutic aspect of the relationship.

3.5 Unconditionality

Barrett-Lennard (1962) defined unconditionality as the degree of constancy of regard felt by one person for another who communicates self-experience to him. The counsellor cares for the client in a non-possessive rather than a conditional way. He does not accept the client only when he is behaving in certain ways. Unconditionality means acceptance without reservations and without evaluations. Hollis (1949) emphasizes this aspect when she states that the counsellor 'must not condemn or feel hostile toward a client because of his behaviour, no matter how greatly it may differ from behaviour of which he personally would approve'. She further states that the counsellor must feel genuine warmth, a certain 'outgoingness' to the other person, thus forming a bridge across which help may be given.

Central to a discussion of unconditionality is the distinction between the client as a person and the client's behaviour. The counsellor manifests a basic respect, concern, and warmth towards the person of the client regardless of his behaviour in or out of the counselling relationship. Hamilton (1948), speaking of the dynamics of unconditionality, says that 'this attitude can come only from respect for people and a genuine desire to help anyone who is in need or trouble. It is translated into courtesy, patience, willingness to listen in a non-critical way to whatever the client may complain of, request, or reveal about himself.'

Unconditionality does not imply that the counsellor is unaffected by the behaviour of the client. He may agree personally with some views and behaviour of the client while disagreeing with others. But, across this spectrum of response, there is a basic respect, concern and caring for the client as a person. Without this the counsellor could not help the client and the client would not continue the relationship. This underlying awareness and respect for the personality of the client enables the counsellor to become a significant person to the client.

Unconditionality, by its very nature, is opposed to the diagnostic practice of labelling. Being labelled can have undesirable effects on the life of the person. While some specific aspect of the person's behaviour leads to labelling, in practice it is the total person who is labelled and who is then reacted to in terms of that label. Ullman and Krasner (1975) state that 'all the negative concepts, many of them demonstrably erroneous, held about members of the class are ascribed to the labelled individual.' It is extremely difficult for the individual to accept himself when he is obtaining such negative feedback from his environment.

Rogers (1954) equates acceptance and unconditionality. 'By acceptance I mean a warm regard for him as a person of unconditional self-worth, of value no matter what his condition, his behaviour or his feelings.' The counsellor then accepts the client unconditionally to the extent that he feels an acceptance of all aspects of the client and his experiences. Standal (1954) used the term 'unconditionality' to emphasize that there are no conditions attached to the acceptance of the other person.

The counsellor should actually experience unconditionality. It is not enough that he should hold abstract attitudes of respect and acceptance of the dignity and worth of the client. Obviously, this experience cannot exist until there is a basis for it in the client-counsellor relationship. Hence, with each new client, the attitude of unconditionality must be created anew.

Tyler (1953) identifies two components of acceptance. The first is a willingness to allow individuals to differ from each other in all sorts of ways, and the second is 'a realization that the ongoing experience of each person is a complex pattern of striving, thinking and feeling'. Unconditionality is a direct outgrowth of the counsellor's ability to be nonjudgemental. He does not manifest normative or judgemental standards against which clients are matched, balanced and found wanting as persons. He does not assign conditions to be met before he will extend his help. Acceptance does not involve either approval or disapproval of the particular aspects of a client's personality or conduct upon which he happens to be reporting at any given time. The counsellor accepts the personality of the client as a whole, not just any one facet of it.

Truax (1962) equates unconditionality with unconditional warmth, which, he claims, requires a nonpossessive caring for the client as a separate person with the inherent right and responsibility of self-determination. The Rogerians, unlike representatives of other approaches, have emphasized warmth as an important variable in counselling. The experience of warmth by the client expresses the acceptance of the counsellor and this in itself will ensure progress. Braatov (1954) sees warmth as the core of therapy. 'Therapies,' he claims, 'are based on the changes which occur in a person where he is given the chance to unburden himself in the presence of another, healthier, more independent individual. The process will never begin unless the therapist from the beginning has a surplus of warmth.'

Rausch and Bordin (1957) distinguish three components of warmth — commitment, effort to understand and spontaneity. Commitment is the degree of willingness of the counsellor to be of assistance to the client. This may vary in degree of activity or concreteness. For example, the counsellor may offer help in collaborating actively with the client in the solution of an external problem, or he may offer help only in a passive way. The counsellor shows his effort to understand the client, firstly, by asking questions designed to elicit the client's view of himself, second- ly, by testing with the client the over-all validity of the impressions that he, the counsellor, has gained from these views, and thirdly, by indicating, by comments or other forms of intervention, his interest in understanding the client's views. These two aspects of warmth would appear to be valuable factors in the establishment of unconditionality.

Unconditionality allows the client to be himself without facade. This eliminates the fear of conditionality. In conditional relationships one is cared for because of one's merit or because one deserves it, and this always leaves the doubt that this care may disappear if its conditions are not met. The experience of unconditionality by the client is a passive one. There is nothing he has to do or can do to deserve it. Unconditionality, then, is an attitude, an orientation of the counsellor towards his client. It is an unconditional affirmation of the worth of the client. It requires altruism on the part of the counsellor. This selfless care is perhaps the most difficult condition required in the counselling relationship. Yet it greatly facilitates client self- disclosure because, irrespective of the content of that disclosure, the client is guaranteed respect and care. It alone allows the client to regress or to engage in the overt expression of whatever he is experiencing at this period in his life. This is important since only to the extent that it occurs can the counsellor empathise with the client, meet him at the level of his present experiencing and aid him in his movement toward self-acceptance and acceptance of others.

3.6 Research Findings
Research findings concerning the counselling relationship will be discussed under the following headings:

(1) Empathy.
(2) Empathy, congruence and unconditional positive regard.
(3) Empathy, congruence, unconditionality and level of regard.

Empathy appears to be the only variable which has been investigated in isolation from the other three. In Roger's study of congruence and unconditional positive regard, empathy was also considered. Barrett-Lennard, keeping his distinction between unconditionality and level of regard, included a consideration of empathy and congruence in his research.

3.6.1 Empathy
Research findings indicate that a high degree of empathy is associated with various aspects of progress in therapy, irrespective of how the construct was measured. Tausch (1969) and his associates related the therapist's level of empathy to both client self-exploration and client improvement; the higher the therapist level of empathy, the higher was the client's level of self-exploration and degree of improvement.

Sander et al. (1968) found that when therapist empathy was lowered, it caused a decrease in patient self-exploration and when it was raised, a rise in patient self-exploration occurred. Truax and Mitchell (1971), in a study of fourteen neurotic clients, discovered that there was a significant relationship between the client's perception of the therapist's empathic behaviour and constructive change in the client. Even more striking, high levels of empathy were found to elicit faster as well as greater client self-exploration. This finding may have important implications where the opportunity for psychotherapy and counselling is limited.

Rogers (1961), in a study of schizophrenics, discovered that the patients receiving the highest degree of empathy in the therapeutic relationship showed the greatest reduction in pathology. This suggests that the sensitive understanding of the therapist may have been the most potent element in bringing the schizophrenic out of his alienation and into the world of relatedness. Jung (1928) said that the schizophrenic ceases to be schizophrenic when he encounters someone by whom he feels understood. Rogers' study provides empirical evidence in support of this statement.

Truax (1963) selected randomly 384 samples of tape-recorded psychotherapy sessions in various stages in the first six months of therapy. These were then coded so that raters would not know whether a sample came from a test-improved case or a test-deteriorated case or from an early or late interview. The findings indicated clearly the relevance of empathy to the kind of personality improvement occurring in the patient. Test-improved patients rated consistently higher on empathy than test-deteriorated cases. In a second study of empathy, Truax investigated trends in the levels of empathy for schizophrenics, covering a time span from six months to three and a half years. One four-minute tape-recorded sample was taken from every fifth interview for each of the fourteen schizophrenic cases, giving a total of 358 samples with which to work. Analysis of the data showed no tendency for therapists to change systematically over time in the level of empathy offered to the patient.

When psychotherapists of many different orientations describe their concept of the ideal therapist, they give empathy the highest ranking out of twelve variables. This result is based on a study by Raskin (1974) of 83 practising therapists of at least eight different therapeutic approaches. Raskin's study corroborated and strengthened earlier research by Fiedler (1950). We may conclude that therapists recognize that the most important factor in being a therapist is endeavouring as sensitively and as accurately as one can to understand the client from the latter's point of view.

Tausch (1973) found that the degree of empathy which exists and will exist in the relationship can be measured very early, sometimes in the fifth but even as early as the second interview. Furthermore such early measurements were predictive of the later success or lack of success in therapy. The implication of these findings is that a great deal of unsuccessful therapy could be avoided by measuring the therapist's empathy early in the relationship.

The study of Halpern (1955) indicated that a person can empathize significantly better in personality areas where he is satisfied with his own behaviour as opposed to areas where he is not satisfied. We may infer from this that a person who is at home with most of his own behaviour is likely to be a relatively good empathiser and consequently a good therapist. This agrees with the findings of Wolf and Murray (1947) that subjects were most accurate in predicting the behaviour of people whose average self-ratings were most similar to their own and least accurate in estimates of those whose average ratings were least similar. They concluded that 'the best explanation seems to be that man can only understand what he has already experienced. He can best empathize with those whose responses resemble his own'. Stotland and Dunn (1963) obtained findings which confirmed this.

Bergin and Jasper (1969) investigated the relationship between therapist personal characteristics and therapist empathy levels during non-client-centred psychotherapy. They concluded that (a) there is a moderate inverse relationship between therapist Minnesota Multiphasic Personality Inventory disturbance levels and the degree of therapist empathy in interviews, (b) there is no correlation between indices of therapists' intellectual ability or academic achievement and their empathy scores, and (c) there is some reason to doubt that judge-rated empathy scores are related to therapy success in non-client-centred therapy.

The lack of relationship between empathy and indices of academic and intellectual competence is not surprising. It simply reaffirms the almost universally held view that scholastic abilities are not very relevant to effectiveness in establishing therapeutic relationships with clients. Their lack, however, may be critical below a certain low level rarely found among graduate counsellors.

Luchins (1950, 1951) found that certain factors tended to interfere with an individual's understanding of another individual. These factors are: centering on one's own needs, emotions or purposes; focusing only on one feature of an individual's behaviour; having stereotyped ideas concerning the relationship between physical features and personality traits; having prejudices regarding an individual's race, religion or nationity. Luchins drew two conclusions from these studies. (1) A person's understanding of another seems to depend on himself, on the other, and on field conditions. (2) Empathic ability is amenable to training. This concurs with Aspy's (1972) finding that the art of empathising can be learnt from empathic persons. The capacity for empathy, Mullen and Abeles (1972) and Fiedler (1950) suggest, is something which can be developed with time and appropriate experience.

Dymond (1952), Baker and Black (1955), Bell and Hall (1954), Halpern (1955), Jackson and Carr (1955), Lesser (1959) and Lundy (1956) conducted a series of studies that dealt with emphatic responses. They asked whether empathic responses are measurable and whether they can be learned. It was implied in their assumptions that most normal individuals possess empathy to a certain degree and that the individual's empathic qualities or characteristics seem to be developed in stages. Dymond's finding that empathy is possessed in different degrees by different people seems conclusive. Dymond, Huges and Raabe (1952) also furnish evidence that the development of empathy is a result of particular life experiences.

Dymond (1948) investigated the relationship of insight and empathy. She defined insight as the intellectual and emotional realization by the subject of the circumstances and relationships out of which his symptoms arose. The therapist, therefore, attempts to give the patient a relatively objective understanding of the interpersonal relationships which were and are important to him, and their relation to his emotional responses and behaviour. The personality of the client is an aggregate of self-other patterns which have been internalized from his previous interactions with others. Insight, therefore, is the understanding of the self-other patterns which the individual has incorporated and which form the basis of his expectations of others, his structuring of his life situation and the place he feels he occupies in it. Dymond studied twenty university student volunteers. The technique used for encouraging and analyzing the self-other patterns on which these students were operating was the TAT. She found that her subjects formed a 'high' and 'low' empathy group. Results revealed that 81 per cent of denied relationships belonged to those of the low empathy group. Since this is so, it appears that empathy is a necessary mechanism for the building up of self-other patterns which are well developed. In the 'low' empathy cases the individual does not project himself into the thoughts and feelings of the other and so does not arrive at a self-other pattern which is well-rounded and which corresponds with the actual relationship. Instead, he builds an inadequate or false representation of the relationship and lacks insight into the fact that he has done this.

Empathic ability appears to be related to and, at least in part, due to the character of the relationships which surrounded the child in the home;

close relationships lead to higher empathic ability than distant ones (Dymond 1948).

These conclusions suggest that empathy may be one of the underlying mechanisms on which insight is based.

Dymond (1950), in a study of eighty students, investigated the personality characteristics of good and poor empathizers. She measured empathy by the ability to predict accurately the self-ratings of others. She found that four factors distinguished the highly empathic group from the less empathic group. These factors were family atmosphere and relationships, orientation to others, life goals, and concept of self.

Highly empathic students came from families in which interpersonal relations were close. The family was a source of support so that they found investing in others to be rewarding. By contrast, the family life of the low empathic group contained a good deal of aggression against parental authority, conflict with siblings, hostility against over-protective mothers, and it also suffered frequently from disrupted relationships through incompatibility between parents or through the death of one of them.

Dymond also found that highly empathic people are warm, outgoing and optimistic. Their own level of security is such that they can afford an interest in others. The low empathic group mistrust others and insulate themselves against them. They seem to compensate for their lack of emotional development by stressing the abstract intellectual approach to life as the safest. They are often egocentric in their relationships, using other people for their own purposes because of the feelings of power and status it gives them. They need to dominate the other in most relationships. They have few friends and find it hard to make friends. They are 'takers' rather than 'givers'.

In terms of goals, the main goal of the highly empathic person could be summed up as seeking to establish a close, mutually interdependent relationship. The goals of the less empathic person, on the other hand, were more in terms of self-aggrandisement and social eminence.

Dymond's research holds implications for the selection of counsellors. It suggests that counselling trainees should be people who, in their ordinary relationships, are warm, generous, understanding and optimistic.

3.6.2 Empathy, Congruence and Unconditional Positive Regard

To determine the relevance of empathy, congruence and unconditional positive regard, Truax (1963) conducted research on fourteen schizophrenics receiving therapy and fourteen matched controls. Patients receiving high levels of empathy, congruence and unconditional positive regard

showed an overall gain in psychological functioning which was mani-
fested in a lowering of anxiety levels. Truax's research seems to point
clearly to the importance of empathy, unconditional positive regard and
congruence in successful psychotherapy with one of the most difficult
patient groups - the hospitalised schizophrenics. Rogers (1965) showed
that schizophrenic patients perceive a much lower level of these attitudes
than do most neurotic clients, although the therapists were manifesting
the same attitudes with each group. This would seem to indicate that
the more disturbed person can less easily perceive and trust the positive
attitudes of another. The more clearly the schizophrenic patients were
able to perceive these attitudes in the relationship, the greater degree of
self-experiencing and self-exploration they exhibited. Finally, the more
satisfactory the relationship in therapy, the more likely it is that the client
will show openness in a relationship with his therapist. Thus, when empathy, congruence and unconditional positive regard are present in therapy
or counselling to a high degree, an overall improvement in personal adjustment seems likely to follow.

In a 1958 study based on twenty tape-recorded cases, ten of which
could be classed by several objective criteria as more successful and ten of
them categorized as less successful, Halkides found that a high degree
of the three conditions was significantly associated with the more successful cases. These high ratings were not associated more significantly with
units from earlier sections. This would indicate that these conditions are
established rapidly and endure over a period — that is to say, the empathic
and congruent counsellor with high unconditional positive regard is so
throughout the counselling process and is so perceived by the client.

Martin, Carkhuff and Berenson (1966) investigated the differences
between counsellors and 'best friends' of clients on empathy, unconditional positive regard and congruence. The clients were sixteen college students, and the two counsellors had over five years of clinical experience.
Each client was interviewed by a counsellor and by his best friend. Following the interviews, the clients completed questionnaires on the empathy,
unconditional positive regard, and congruence of the counsellor and friend,
and on their own self- exploration in the interviews. In addition, three
trained graduate students rated these variables on Truax and Carkhuff's
five-point scale, using three four-minute excerpts from each taped interview. The counsellors differed significantly from the friends on all rated
variables. Differences on these traits measured by the questionnaire scores
were significant except for the client self-exploration variable. The counsellors obtained a mean of 3, claimed by Carkhuff to be the minimal level
of facilitative functioning; the friends obtained a score of 2. There were

differences between the two counsellors on the four counsellor variables. This study points to the importance of training and experience in these variables since the counsellors obtained higher ratings on facilitative conditions than did the friends.

Truax and Carkhuff (1965) studied the effect of manipulating therapeutic conditions within one therapeutic hour upon the intrapersonal exploration of three hospitalized female schizophrenics. During the first twenty minutes a baseline level of the patient's intrapersonal exploration was established with the use of a ten-point scale. The therapist was then interrupted. For the next twenty minutes of the interview he 'deliberately' lowered his empathic understanding and unconditional positive regard for the patient by giving negative non- verbal cues. For the final twenty minutes he acted normally. Congruence was not altered during the entire interview. Empathy, unconditional positive regard and congruence were measured by the respective scale ratings of fifteen three-minute samples from each of the three therapeutic sessions. Analysis of the data indicated that these conditions were lowered during the experimental middle third of the interview as intended. These changes in therapist-offered conditions served to lower the patient's depth of self-exploration.

3.6.3 Empathy, Congruence, Unconditionality and Level of Regard
The study of Gross and De Ridder (1966) provided evidence that congruence, empathy, unconditionality and level of regard were significantly associated with client improvement in comparatively short-term counselling. The rank order correlations were (a) congruence with improvement .82: (b) empathy with improvement .75: (c) unconditionality with improvement .83 . Level of regard was the only relationship variable which did not reach significance. These findings would seem to support our earlier hypothesis that level of regard is of relative rather than absolute importance in the counselling relationship.

Barrett- Lennard (1962) administered the Relationship Inventory to forty-two clients after the fifth interview and again at the termination of therapy. He found that those clients who eventually showed more therapeutic change, perceived more empathy, congruence, unconditionality and level of regard after the fifth interview than did those who showed less change. Where the client perceived these qualities in the relationship early in therapy, the prognosis was good. Barrett-Lennard also ascertained that those clients who were better adjusted at the beginning of therapy tend to perceive more of these therapeutic conditions in the relationship than do those clients who are less well adjusted.

The same author compared a group of more experienced with less experienced therapists and discovered that the clients of the former were aware of more of the therapeutic conditions than were the clients of the latter. This seems to suggest that, as the therapists grow more skillful, they are better able to experience and to provide the conditions for effective therapy. On the other hand, these conditions can have an effective therapeutic input only to the extent that the client is aware of them, and to some degree his capacity for awareness depends on his adjustment. Barrett-Lennard further maintains that there are 'good' therapists and 'good' clients with regard to the ability to respond well to the four variables. The combination of the 'good' client and therapist would imply an excellent prognosis for therapy. A poor therapist paired with a poor client would be unlikely to produce high levels of the variables. A good client paired with a poor therapist may perceive the response positively and have a productive therapeutic experience, while a good therapist with a poor client may ultimately succeed in communicating the qualities of the four variables and thus help the client. These suggestions provide interesting hypotheses for further research.

Hollenbeck (1965), in an investigation of the relationships of fifty men and fifty women with their parents, hypothesized that high levels of congruence, empathy, level of regard and unconditionality would be positively related to adjustment. He found that only one of the conditions, namely unconditionality of regard, failed consistently to relate to the adjustment criterion. This suggests that the importance of unconditionality in the parent-child relationship is not the same as in the developing counselling relationship. For the sub-sample of women, level of regard and congruence in the father relationship were significantly related to adjustment, while for the men, congruence in the father relationship was the only condition significantly related to adjustment.

In 1967, Truax and Wargo studied 160 hospitalized patients in twenty-four sessions over a three-month period and found that patients who improved significantly had received high levels of empathy, unconditionality and congruence. They reported similar findings for a group of eighty institutionalised juvenile delinquents, who received three months of group counselling. Replicating the same basic design and study on a sample of eighty outpatients receiving group psychotherapy in 1969, they found that unconditionality, in particular, and congruence to a slightly lesser extent, were more critical to patient improvement than empathy. From their study of forty outpatients treated in individual psychotherapy, Truax et al (1966) observed a greater improvement on two overall measures in patients seen by therapists offering high levels of empathy, unconditionality and congruence than in-patients receiving relatively lower levels of the combined conditions. Further analyses showed identical findings for empathy and congruence, but a reversed tendency for unconditionality.

These findings hold true for a wide variety of clients, counsellors and therapeutic contexts.

4

Core Outcomes: *Theory and Research*

4.1 Core Outcomes

It is suggested in chapter 2 that the goal of counselling is 'healing'. Having identified the goal in general terms, the problem then becomes the operationalization of the concept so that we may select or construct appropriate measuring tools.

Rogers (1951, 1961) indicates that the therapeutic outcome must be operationalized in terms of change in the client's concept of himself and in his self-acceptance. 'There has been a stress upon the acceptance of self as one of the outcomes of therapy. We have established the fact that in successful psychotherapy negative attitudes towards the self decrease and positive attitudes increase.' (Rogers 1961) and again 'it would appear that the individual in successful therapy tends to perceive all aspects of self and self-in-relationship with less emotion and more objectivity.' (Rogers, 1951).

An understanding of the notion of 'self' both as a theoretical entity and an empirical variable is fundamental if we are to use the client's perception and acceptance of self as a measure of therapeutic outcome.

4.2 The Self

Man, for a long time, has been aware of the value and significance of self-knowledge. In ancient Greece, the entrance to the temple of Apollo at Delphi bore the inscription 'Know Thyself', and in Homeric literature the concept of self is depicted. Shakespeare, in a much later age, gave wise advice to humanity through the mouth of Polonius when he admonished Laertes: 'This above all, to thine own self be true, and it follows as the night the day, thou cans't not then be false to any man.'

The term 'self', with its many meanings and its wide range of applications, reaches to the very roots of language and of human nature. In modern psychology, however, the concept came to prominence with the discussion of William James (1890) and also that of the Germans, Lipps (1883), Müller–Freienfels (1936), and Österreich (1910) [cf. Dempsey (1975)].

Lipps (1883), in the early days of experimental psychology, declared that the content of consciousness is referred to a primary 'I'. Müller-Freienfels (1936) believed that the self is involved in every mental act. 'This fact,' he says, 'is borne out by language usage such as "I sense," "I think," and the like.' Österreich (1910) stated that in phenomena such as perceiving, judging and feeling, we cannot evade the question: 'Who is perceiving, judging and feeling?' 'The only answer that can be given,' he says, 'is that an 'I' is perceiving and the 'I' in every person is identical with that person's self.'

James (1890) distinguished in the self the two aspects of 'I' and 'me'. 'The "I",' he said, 'is the self as observer or knower, the self that perceives the real world and reacts to it. The 'me' is the self as observed, as an object. This 'me' he regarded as consisting of whatever the individual views as belonging to himself, a material self, a social self and a spiritual self. In the tradition of James, Dempsey (1975) distinguished a body self, a social self, a cognitive self and an affective self.

Writing at approximately the same time as James, Titchener (1896), following Wundt (1894), declared that the self is 'the sum total of conscious processes which run their course under conditions laid down by bodily conditions'. The Gestalt School took a different view. Koffka (1935) declared that:

'In a science (psychology) which, for such a long time, has done all it could to disparage the idea of an ego, it is not easy to appraise justly the importance of our concept of the enduring ego system. It may exert a far greater influence on the whole body of psychology than we can see at present.'

Koffka believed that the ego gave a real basis for the scientific understanding of the development of the personality.

In contrast to both Wundt and Titchener and the Gestalt school of experimental psychology, the great pioneers of clinical psychology had a somewhat different outlook on the 'ego' and the 'self'. For Freud (1923), the ego was the psychic agency which organises experiences, cognitive impressions, images of external reality and emotional reactions. It is conscious but has preconscious and even unconscious aspects. Jung (1928) saw the individuated self as involving an awareness and acceptance of one's unique nature, one's consciousness and unconsciousness of the heights and the depths, the good and the bad, of the irrational and chaotic as well as of the rational and creative, of thinking as well as feeling, of sensation as well as intuition. The individuated self, for Jung, brings with it an awareness and acceptance of living and of all life. Adler (1923) believed that the unitary, consistent, creative self was sovereign. The creative self constructs the person out of the raw material of heredity and experience. It is the yeast that acts upon the facts of the world and transforms them into a personality that is subjective, dynamic, unified and uniquely stylised. The creative self gives meaning to life; it creates the goal, as well as the means to the goal. It is the active principle of human living.

Along with Adler, whose awareness of the significance of social structure and social forces in the development of the self distinguished him from Freud and Jung, can be placed two sociologists, Charles Horton Cooley and George Mead. Cooley (1902) put forward the looking-glass theory of the self. He believed that through interaction with others and through the use of language, an individual comes to think of himself as 'I'. As he perceives the attitudes of others towards this 'I', he develops a self-image. He takes on a view of himself from observing the way others respond to him. Hence, he spoke of the looking-glass self. The behaviour of others towards him is the mirror in which the individual sees himself. For Mead (1934), the self arises from the process of social interaction and communication, especially linguistic communication which makes it possible to replace behaviour with ideas and words. The self, insofar as it is active, (1) is free, (2) has initiative and uniqueness and (3) is the product and container of internal traditions, values and attitudes.

Up to about 1920, psychologists regarded the self as an important concept. Then, under the influence of the behaviourism of Pavlov, Watson and Skinner, it became unfashionable and unscientific to refer to it. With the elimination of human experience as a reputable object of study and with the limiting of psychology to the consideration of observable behaviour, the concept of the self largely disappeared from academic psychological discussion. The revival of interest was due primarily to the work of Gordon Allport who gave a new direction to the psychology of his time with his work on Personality (1949) and on Becoming (1955). This led Hilgard, in 1949, to choose for his presidential address to the American Psychological Association, the theme that the concept of self was essential for understanding defense mechanisms. At this time too, Litwinski (1951) stated: 'Recognition that the search for the self is a significant scientific endeavour seems to be increasing'. Sullivan, in 1953, agreed that the concept of the self was significant, stressing, like Cooley and Mead, that it arose out of social interactions with significant others, particularly with the mother.

During the past twenty years, psychologists have been increasingly concerned with devising ways and means of operationalizing the theoretical construct of 'self'. Because of its complexity, any attempt to measure it adequately must be multi-faceted. Over the years the main facets which have been investigated are the self-concept (Raimy 1948, Videbeck 1960, Deutsch and Solomon 1959), the ideal self (Medinnus 1961, Clifford and Clifford 1967, Hanlon, Hofstaetter and O'Connor), self-acceptance (Coopersmith 1967, Hamachek 1971, McCandless 1967), and self-other acceptance (Stock 1949, Sheerer 1949, Phillips 1951, Berger 1953, Fey 1955). A discussion of each of these variables follows.

4.3 The Self-concept

Self-concept can be described as a person's awareness of himself. Brownfain (1952), implying that an individual has his own unique way of perceiving himself, describes it as a system of central meanings that a person has concerning himself and his relations to the world around him. For O' Hara and Tiedman (1959), it is the individual's evaluation of himself.

The self- concept is closely related to behaviour. Rogers (1951) claimed that most of the ways of behaving adopted by a human organism are those consistent with the concept of the self. Ziller (1973) and Shranger (1975) likewise believe that a person's self-concept affects his behaviour in social and non-social situations. Lecky (1945) maintained that a person's behaviour is an effort to maintain the integrity, unity and inner consistency of the personality system which has as its nucleus the individual's evaluation of himself.

When a person is in a situation where he might learn something contrary to what he already believes about himself, he will tend to protect himself by not perceiving the information or by distorting it so that it appears less threatening. This is particularly true of the insecure person. The insecure individual often preserves his self-concept by forming a low opinion of his critics. For example, when children at school are scolded by a disliked teacher, they can maintain a brave image of personal competence by categorising the teacher as 'nasty' or in some other unfavourable way.

Secure people, on the other hand, can receive feedback about themselves without stress. Such feedback serves two functions — it informs and it motivates. It is a mechanism whereby a person can monitor his own behaviour, the impact he makes on others and the success or failure of his own efforts. Feedback is more likely to be welcomed if it is first sought by the person. If it is offered to a person without any prior indication from him that he wants it, feedback will tend to be rejected.

The individual's perception of his own feelings, attitudes and ideas, according to Moustakas (1956), can be more valid than that of another. This statement is true insofar as a normal individual can know what is going on consciously in his mind. But there may be values at work in his personality and attitudes influencing his behaviour of which he is not aware, but which may be quite perceptible to others. A person develops a concept of himself as a result of both his self-perceptions and the feedback he receives from those around him.

The precept 'Know thyself' suggests that self-knowledge is not something that man possesses inherently but something that he may acquire, or for which he has to strive. Murphy (1947) and Sullivan (1947) state that a person's self-concept develops as his abilities and tendencies, his entire psycho-physiological structure encounters the impact of life's experiences. Man alone has the power of understanding, of evaluating, of forming and moulding himself. Man alone is responsible for what he has become, for what he is.

Man's concept of himself is not necessarily accurate. The self-concept, to quote Raimy (1948), may have little or no relationship to reality. 'A person is often surprised by his own actions, often amazed by the strange fantasies that haunt his mind and by the bizarre behaviour that follows in their wake.' A person may also be relatively unaware of the real motives underlying his behaviour. He may believe a certain action to be unselfish and suddenly realise that it is prompted by very egotistical motives.

Frequently a person does not know what others think of him. When he becomes aware of their opinion he may not believe it to be true, especially if it does not conform to what he thinks or if it is uncomplimentary. Moreover, when he is emotionally disturbed, his perception of assessments of himself by others may be distorted.

Yet such evaluation does actually influence the self-concept. For Sullivan (1953), Rogers (1961) and Lecky (1945), the self-concept depends, in large measure, upon the reactions of others and their expressed evaluation.

Videbeck (1960) deduced experimentally that the self-concept could be changed through manipulation of the type of evaluation of an individual given by others. He suggested that evaluations influence the self-concept relative to the number of times a particular evaluation is made, the appropriateness or qualifications of the person making it, the strength of the motivation of the subject criticized with respect to the evaluated attributes and the intensity with which the approval or disapproval is expressed. His subjects were thirty students who had been assigned on a random basis to one of two conditions: approval or disapproval with respect to speaking ability. All those involved rated themselves equally prior to the experimental treatment. After the evaluation session, the self-concepts of those in the approval group became more positive while the self-concepts of the subjects in the disapproval group became more negative.

4.4 The Ideal Self

The concept of an ideal self is closely related to the Freudian ego-ideal which has its origin in the child's identification with people whom he loves, admires, or fears. Through the process of identification, the child incorporates and imitates the values and attitudes of those around him. His parents are the first and most important objects of identification. The behaviour of which they approve and for which they reward him tends to become incorporated into his ego-ideal. In the adult the ego-ideal is the dynamic composite of the identifications the individual has achieved.

Murray (1953) regarded the ego-ideal as an idealized picture of the aspiring self, a set of personal ambitions toward which the individual strives. For him, one of the important features of personality is the ego-ideal, an integration of images which portrays the person at his future best, realizing all his ambitions. Murray's conception of the ego-ideal provides more latitude for changes and development in the years subsequent to childhood than does the orthodox psychoanalytic view. It is also clear that Murray equates the ego-ideal and the ideal self.

Social psychologists hold a somewhat similar view. They regard the term 'ideal self' as a name for the integrated set of roles and aspirations which direct the individual's life. These roles and aspirations, they believe, are taken on by the individual from parents, older siblings, playmates, teachers and other persons to whom he is attracted and who appear to him to be endowed with superiority and prestige.

Jourard (1958) defined the self-ideal as a set of beliefs which an individual holds concerning how he should behave.

'These specifications of ideal behaviour ultimately derive from the more abstract moral and ethical precepts or values current within society. The individual may formulate these values as either abstract propositions of right or wrong or as very specific prescriptions and formulae which prescribe how he should behave in various situations. If his values have been acquired in the context of an authoritarian relationship, the ideal self becomes a rigid structure, strongly resistant to change. In fact, when confronted with social pressure to change his values, he may obstinately resist all such external pressures. He finds it difficult to examine, criticize and alter his values because they come from sources he dares not question — his parents and teachers. He does not wish to examine his values in the light of critical reason. He will reject or ignore all criticism of the self-ideal.'

A close association can exist between the ideal self and guilt. Guilt is a reaction to failure to behave as one thinks one should. Since the ideal self refers to a person's concept of how he should act, it provides a standard in terms of which the individual appraises his own conduct. When a person has acquired values or ideals which are well out of the range of his capacity to implement, he has prepared the groundwork for a feeling of chronic guilt. On the other hand, if he behaves in accordance with values within his range, he will experience self-esteem and believe that he is a worthwhile, likeable and acceptable person.

What is possible to attain may, however, be difficult and demand effort and sacrifice. Discipline forces the parent to remind the child of discrepancies between what he is and what he ought to be. Medinnus (1961), in a study of fathers and mothers in a small community, using Q-sort descriptions of their five-year-old children, found that there was considerable discrepancy between parents' idealised pictures of their children and their observations of the children's actual behaviour. If the real-ideal coefficients can be interpreted as the degree to which the parents accept a child's behaviour, then it seems that there is but moderate acceptance of it. However, it is also possible to infer that the parent may simply be noting characteristics, which in his judgement would make life more serene and happy for his child. The child who notices that there is a discrepancy between his parents' perception of him and what they would like him to be, comes to view this discrepancy as a reproach, rather than a source of inspiration. As he develops, the ideals projected for him by significant others come gradually to assume the form of moral absolutes which he adopts as standards of behaviour.

For Havighurst, Robinson and Dorr (1946), the ideal self commences in childhood in identification with a parental figure. It moves through a stage of romanticism and glamour in middle childhood and early adolescence as a composite of characteristics embodied in an actual, visible, attractive adult or in a fictional, imaginary one. After the child has reached the age of eight years, these authors maintain, parents or those of their generation play a diminishing role in the ideal self. Between 10 and 15, glamorous non-parental adults are important. Youngsters over 15 who report a glamour figure as their ideal are, they say, probably immature, measured by standards of development common to a big majority of this age group.

It must be noted, however, that environment, particularly lower social economic status, makes for slower developmental progress at the 'glamorous' identification stage around 15. Children who are surrounded by powerful prestigious adults visibly capable of obtaining the desirable things of life, transcend more quickly this 'glamour' phase of development.

Clifford and Clifford (1976), in an investigation of boys aged between 16 and 21, found that ideal self measures showed little or no change over that time. This may suggest either that by then the ideal self has become rather stable and relatively resistant to change, or that the experience of this group has had little or no effect upon their concept of the ideal self.

Mowrer (1953), Rogers (1951), Seeman and Raskin (1953) have demonstrated an increase in the correlation between the client's self-concept and his ideal self-concept as measured by Rogers' Q-sort. Hanlon, Hofstaetter and O'Connor (1954), using the California Test of Personality and a modified Q-sort technique, found that the correlation between the self-concept and the ideal self tends to be positive .33 to .46. The over-all tendency therefore is towards a congruence of the self-concept and the ideal self. This is corroborated by the study of Payne, Drummond and Lunghi (1970) who administered personality and self-concept measures to 35 male school-leavers of an Arctic training expedition both prior to their departure and upon their return. The results showed that there was a significant reduction in the discrepancy between the self-description and the ideal self-description by the end of the expedition. This would indicate that the achievement felt on completion of the expedition led either to an increase in self-concept scores or to a reduction of self-ideal scores, or a little of both.

The discrepancy between the quantitative scoring of a given characteristic on the self scale and the ideal scale has been taken by Butler and Haigh (1954) as indicating the way in which an individual perceives himself as possessing this characteristic and the degree to which he values this trait. Successful therapy should, it would seem from this, be accompanied by a reduction in the magnitude of self-concept/self-ideal discrepancies. Turner and Vanderlippe (1958) hypothesise that, as a result of therapy, self-concepts change more than ideal concepts. These expectations have been confirmed by Butler and Haigh (1954). On the other hand, a large discrepancy between the way a person actually sees himself and the way he would ideally like to be can indicate a highly self-critical attitude. Very self-critical people are less well adjusted than those who are at least moderately satisfied with themselves. McCandless (1967) showed that people experience conflict about the traits on which they have the greatest self-concept/self-ideal discrepancy. He also maintained that the evidence for a curvilinear relation between self-concept and self-ideal discrepancy and adjustment is not clear. The reason for this is that, while actual self-concept measures distribute themselves on a normal curve from very negative to very positive, ideal self-concepts are generally socially stereotyped. Thus, most of the information to be gained from computing a discrepancy score is already present in the variation of the self-concept score. If a wide range of self-concept scores is subtracted from a relatively constant set of ideal self-concept scores, the resulting distribution of the discrepancy scores is closely correlated with the original distribution of the self-concept scores.

Rogers and Dymond (1954) believe that self-ideal/self-concept discrepancy is unhealthy and one of their goals in therapy is to reduce this discrepancy. This may be done by raising the self-concept or lowering the level of an impossibly high ideal self, or both. Katz and Zigler (1967), however, view the whole question from a slightly different perspective. For them, the higher the maturity level the greater the individual's capacity for incorporating social demands, mores and values. The highly developed person makes greater demands upon himself. He is more often unable to fulfill them and consequently may experience more guilt than the less developed person. The former has more differentiating ability which results in a greater awareness of the disparity between his real and his ideal self. From their study of a group of 120 largely middle-class children, 40 each from fifth, eighth and eleventh grades, the authors found that the older and brighter children showed greater self-ideal/self-concept discrepancies than the younger or the lower IQ children. This would seem to bear out their hypothesis that more mature people make greater self-demands.

McKenna, Hofstaetter and O'Connor (1956), from an investigation of ninety 19–20 year old female college students, concluded that the self-ideal has to be considered as factorially complex. The ideal self is a composite of the traits which we accept in ourselves and which we esteem highly in others. Komarovsky (1946) found that many female college seniors are acutely aware of the difficulties involved in attempting to live up to the divergent ideals embodied in their own and their parents' expectations. This agrees with the Freudian emphasis on the role of significant others in the development of our ideal selves.

In an investigation of males over 65 years of age, Dimmit (1959) ascertained that they tend to see their past self-concept as congruent with their ideal self-concept. He suggested that men of this age are involved with their past for two reasons: (1) Western culture is youth orientated and in it youth is valued very highly; (2) Men of approximately 65 years of age tend, in our culture, to be respected for what they used to be rather than for what they presently are.

4.5 Self-acceptance

Self-acceptance is the ability of the person to accept himself as he really is. For an individual it means accepting the positive aspects of himself and seeing what can be done with the negative. If nothing can be done about the latter, then it involves accepting these also. The moral value of self-acceptance has long been recognised.

Rogers (1961) maintains that the basic challenge of every human life is self-understanding and self-acceptance. Just as an individual must maintain a healthy view of the world around him, so he must learn to perceive himself in positive ways. The importance of self-acceptance can be shown in that it is not the people who feel that they are liked, wanted and accepted who fill our mental hospitals, rather it is those who feel unliked, unwanted and unaccepted.

A person's feelings about himself are learned responses. Sometimes negative feelings have to be unlearned. This may require the help of another person, usually a friend or counsellor so that the possibility of honest evaluation is greater. A person with little or no awareness of personal worth sometimes feels a strong need to condemn himself. May (1953) noted that self-condemnation may be a technique to get a substitute for a sense of worth. Allport (1950) supported this viewpoint when he stated: 'If the individual is self-critical, he may be endeavouring to show how praise-worthy he really is.' Self-condemnation may not be so much an honest statement of one's short-comings as a means of avoiding a confrontation with the possibility that one is not capable. It protects the person from the pain of feeling worthless. May (1953) stated: 'The self-condemning substitute for self-worth provides the individual with a method of avoiding an open and honest confronting of his problems of isolation and worthlessness."

In the literature of psychology, the terms 'self-acceptance' and 'self-esteem' are interchangeable. Hamachek's (1971) definition of self-acceptance is an example. He states that the extent to which a person's self-concept is congruent with his description of his ideal self is a measure of self-acceptance. Similarly Cohen (1956) defines self-esteem as the degree of correspondence between an individual's ideal and actual concept of himself. Myers and Myers' (1976) definition of self-esteem — as the feeling which we get when what we do matches our self-image — is similar to that of Cohen. It is worth noting that in everyday language the term 'self-esteem' refers only to the positive aspects of self-acceptance.

Coopersmith (1967) investigated the conditions which lead an individual to value himself and to regard himself as a person of worth. He found that the antecedents of high self-acceptance were personal warmth, clearly defined limits of personal behaviour and respectful treatment. He further reported that persons high in self-acceptance relate to people with the expectation that they will be well-received and successful, while people low in self-acceptance are more destructive, more anxious and more prone to manifest psychosomatic symptoms.

Hamachek (1971), in his study, found that the high self-accepting person had certain values and principles in which he had a strong belief and which he was willing to defend even in the face of strong group disapproval. However, he felt sufficiently secure to modify them if new experience and evidence suggested that he was in error. He felt equal to others as a person, irrespective of the differences in specific abilities, family backgrounds or attitudes of others towards him. He believed that he was a person of interest to others; he could accept praise and he was able to accept the idea that he was capable of feeling a wide range of impulses and desires. He retained confidence in his ability to deal with problems and he was sensitive to the needs of others.

Diggory (1955) described self- esteem as the craving to think well of oneself. He believed that self-esteem is determined by the ratio of actualities to supposed potentialities. Mead (1934) believed that self-evaluation depends on abilities and capacities as they are realized in the performance of definite functions. Yet, Festinger (1954) pointed out that when we evaluate our acts in terms of their success or failure, there may be a universal 'upward push', with respect to abilities, which weights our evaluations towards the favourable end of the scale in spite of possible evidence that they should be lower. James (1890) holds that self-feelings may maintain a relatively constant level independent of the objective reasons a person may have for satisfaction or discontent. He states that 'the barometer of our self-esteem and confidence may vary with causes that seem to be visceral and organic rather than rational.' Nevertheless, the more usual determination of self-acceptance would appear to be one's actual success or failure and the favourable or unfavourable position one holds in society.

Raimy (1948) postulated that self-approval and self-disapproval represent two ends of a continuum which may be viewed as one of the major dimensions of the self- concept. The approval, disapproval or ambivalence a person feels for his self- concept is related to his personal adjustment. A heavy weighting of disapproval or ambivalence suggests a maladjusted individual since maladjustment inevitably implies distress or disturbance in connection with oneself. The adjusted individual may dislike or disapprove of certain aspects of the self-concept but in general he accepts himself.

McCandless (1967) reviewed twelve studies designed to investigate the psychological consequences of discrepancies between the perceived self and the ideal self. He concluded:

'Most research evidence indicates that people who show a large discrepancy between the way they actually see themselves and the way they would ideally like to be, are less well adjusted than those who are at least moderately satisfied with themselves. Evidence indicates that highly self-critical children and adults are more anxious, more insecure and possibly more cynical and depressed than self-accepting people. They may be more ambitious and driving. There is some question as to whether or not the topic of discrepancy between the self-concept and the self-ideal is really different from the topic of positive and negative self-concepts. It would appear that self-concept/self-ideal discrepancy and self-acceptance are in fact measures of adjustment but that they approach the question of adjustment from slightly different standpoints.'

In a recent investigation, Myers and Myers (1976) studied the relation of verbal patterns to high and low self-acceptance. They found that a low level of self-acceptance can be characterised by a defensiveness about blame, a need to talk about self in terms of criticism, an inability to accept praise gracefully, a cynicism about accomplishments, the use of cliché phrases and a pessimistic attitude towards competition. A high level of self-acceptance, on the other hand, can be characterised by originality of expression, by the absence of a need to talk about self frequently, by the acceptance of praise or blame gracefully, by a confident tone of voice and an optimistic attitude about competition.

Engel (1959) found a relative stability of self-concept in people between the ages of thirteen and seventeen years. She also found that those subjects whose self-concept on first testing was negative were significantly less stable in their self-concept than were those whose initial view of themselves was positive. Furthermore, those who persisted in a negative self-concept showed significantly more maladjustment on the MMPI than than those who persisted in a positive one.

In close accord with these findings are those of Musgrave (1966). He found that self-concepts of sixth formers were far more negative than the self-concepts of first-formers. The discrepancy was greater in the case of boys than of girls. Sixth-form boys made more affectively toned and fewer neutral statments than the first formers, the shift from neutral statements was entirely in the direction of negative statements. The developed critical powers of senior pupils might be held to account for their comparatively unfavourable view of themselves and their schools.

Rosenberg (1965) carried out a study of the correlates of self-esteem in 5,077 adolescents between the ages of 15 and 18. Those who were low in self-esteem reported themselves as shy, easily embarrassed, bothered very much if others had a poor opinion of them, eager for approval and inclined to put up a facade. The also had more psychosomatic symptoms.

4.6 Self-other Acceptance

Adler (1926) recognised a connection between feelings toward oneself and feelings towards others. He believed that a 'tendency to disparage' others arose out of a feeling of inferiority towards oneself. According to Fromm (1939), a failure to accept oneself is accompanied by a basic hostility towards others and arises out of the suppression of the individual's spontaneity or of his real self. Horney (1939) asserted that the person who cannot attribute positive values to himself is incapable of attributing them to others.

According to Rogers (1951), the person who accepts himself will, for that very reason, have better interpersonal relations with others. Stock (1949) found that a definite relationship exists between the way an individual feels about himself and the way he feels about other persons. An individual who holds negative feelings toward himself tends to hold negative feelings toward other people and as his self-regard feelings change to the objective and the positive, feelings about others change in a similar direction.

Fromm-Reichmann (1949) remarked that one can respect others only to the extent that one respects oneself, and that where there is low self-esteem there is low esteem of others and fear of low appreciation by others. In counselling, then, as a person begins to accept himself, he becomes capable of experiencing an accepting attitude towards others. Such changes in acceptance of the self and correlated changes in the acceptance of others occurring during client-centred therapy were studied by Sheerer (1949). She found that in approximately three-quarters of the responses the clients were occupied with self-evaluation while one-fifth of their responses were concerned with the evaluation of others. In general there is a marked and fairly regular increase in the measured acceptance of and respect for self from the beginning to the end of the therapy period. There is also a marked but more uneven rise in the acceptance of others. A substantial correlation exists between the attitudes of acceptance of self and attitudes of acceptance of others. She maintains that acceptance of others is higher in the second half of the counselling interviews than in the first.

Sheerer's study and a similar one by Stock (1949) showed that perceptions of others, feelings towards others and acceptance of others are significantly related to the perception of the self, feelings about the self and acceptance of the self. This research showed that with an increase in self-acceptance there is a corresponding increase in favourable attitude toward others.

Phillips (1951) investigated the extent to which these observations held true for larger populations. He constructed a questionnaire on 'Attitudes toward the self and others' which he administered to several groups of students. In an advanced university class the correlation between attitudes towards the self and attitudes towards others was relatively high (.74), while with a group of younger college students it was lower (.54). Berger (1952) used Sheerer's definitions as the basis for the development of his scale. He found a moderate correlation (.65) between acceptance of self and acceptance of others among evening students and a low correlation (.36) among day students. This agrees with Phillips.

Omwake (1954), in a study of 113 college students, found that there is a consistent tendency for those who accept themselves to accept others and for those who have a low opinion of themselves to reject others. Allen (1942) has expressed a similar viewpoint in his discussions of therapy with children.

McIntyre (1952) used a sociometric method to isolate the most accept-ed and the least accepted groups in a college dormitory. He found that neither self-acceptance nor acceptance of others scores differed significantly between the groups. Fey (1965), however, argued that if neither self-acceptance nor acceptance of others scores form the basis for reliable predictions of personality characteristics of people, their combin-ation may do so. Specifically, he found that expressed attitudes of self-acceptance and acceptance of others tend to vary proportionately. For the persons who are exceptions to this rule, the response patterns appear to reveal their manner of interpersonal defences. Individuals showing low self-acceptance and high acceptance of others appeared to be intropunitive and self-disparaging. Those with high self-acceptance and low acceptance of others were especially resistant to the idea of personal psychotherapy and appeared to be extrapunitive and depreciative of others.

Fey (1955), repeating the McIntyre design, hypothesized that accept-ance of others is partly a function of the pattern of interrelationships between one's attitude toward oneself and attitudes towards others. His subjects were 58 third-year medical students. Analysis of the data indic-ated that individuals with high self-acceptance scores tend also to accept others and to feel accepted by them. Yet, in fact, they were neither more nor less accepted than those with low self-acceptance scores. Individuals with high acceptance of others scores tended, in turn, to feel accepted by others and to be accepted by them. Persons who think better of them-selves than they do of others tend to feel accepted by others, whereas they are significantly less well liked by them. These individuals overestimate significantly their acceptability to others. A comparison of most and least accepted groups showed that the latter have a significantly larger gap between their scores for self-acceptance and acceptance of others.

Persons of high self-acceptance are less susceptible to interpersonal influence in social interaction. They tend to exert more influence than persons of low self-acceptance. Thomas and Burdik (1954) conducted an experiment involving thirty post-graduate students of social psychology. They found that subjects with a high level of self-acceptance were more influential in an interaction situation than those with a low self-acceptance level. Cohen (1956) obtained similar results in an investigation with forty-four undergraduate students. His data indicated that, both in terms of their own perceptions and in terms of their partners' perceptions, high self-acceptance persons have more influence in interaction situations. It is not clear, however, whether the greater impact of the high-acceptance individuals is due to their ability to influence or to the greater responsiveness of the low acceptance group.

In Cohen's study, persons of low self-acceptance showed a negative response to criticism of their performance and to indications of failure communicated to them by members of their social group. Persons, however, with high self-acceptance coped confidently with the experience of criticism in the experimental situation. They accepted and integrated the criticism into their self-concept. Thus an even higher level of self-acceptance was attained.

Manis (1958), in an investigation of the effects of acceptance by others, selected extreme adjustment groups of college students on the basis of certain MMPI scores. He reported that the well-adjusted subjects felt that they were more highly accepted by their parents than did the maladjusted subjects. However, this study does not reveal whether students' perceptions of their parents' feeling toward them are accurate or whether, in the case of the maladjusted sample, the maladjustment was in fact caused by parental attitudes.

Jourard and Remy (1955) stated that for both males and females significant correlations are found between self-acceptance and the perceived attitudes of the parents towards them. Those who evaluate themselves negatively and who believe that their parents evaluate them negatively are more insecure. As in the investigation of Manis, the actual attitudes of the parents may or may not correspond to the perceptions of the children. Hence, if a person believes that his parents approve of his traits, even though they do not, he himself will tend to approve of those traits as well.

On a number of grounds, therefore, one might hypothesize that acceptance of self would be greatest for those who feel that their parents felt positively towards them. In an investigation using eighty-two male school seniors, Suinn (1961) administered Q-sort measures of self-concept and the subjects's perception of his father. A significant positive correlation was found between self-acceptance and acceptance by the father. Rosenberg (1965) also supports this result in his findings.

Maehr, Mensing and Nafzgar (1962) likewise tested the hypothesis that the evaluation expressed by others brings about related changes in the individuals concept of self. They ascertained that the approving and the disapproving reactions of certain 'significant' others were followed by corresponding increases and decreases in the subject's evalution of self.

4.7 The Self-concept in Counselling

In counselling, the self-concept is a primary consideration. However a person may appear to be to an observer, it is how he perceives his 'self', operationalized as his self- concept, which will determine his behaviour. Conversely, the self-concept filters and colours the experience of the individual. Hence, although many of the reasons which bring clients to counselling arise from overt behavioural problems, a resolution of difficulties nearly always centres on an increased understanding of his 'self'.

Counselling seeks to align the self-concept with a more realistic appreciation of the overt and hidden strengths and limitations of the real self. Arnold and Gasson (1954) see this as the goal of counselling. It is the psychologist's practical translation of the philosophical axiom 'Know thyself'. However, it is not sufficient just to know oneself. To know oneself, without accepting what one is, can have a very negative effect on the individual. Thus, in counselling, a greater knowledge of oneself should lead to a greater self-acceptance. As has been mentioned previously, acceptance of others appears to be concomitant with self-acceptance.

This view of counselling, although generally applicable, is particularly relevant in adolescence. Fleege (1945) holds that during adolescence the unfolding of the self 'is making the adolescent ever more aware that he is a person distinct and apart, an individual with personal responsibilities. With every successive experience the idea of his "self" becomes more clearly delineated and he begins to interpret everything in the light of the effect it has on himself. Thus the idea of his "self" comes to occupy the forefront of his consciousness.'

Allport (1946) reinforces this standpoint: 'The sense of "self" (during adolescence) is exceedingly poignant." Within the counselling relationship, the adolescent explores and develops a realistic concept of self. Adolescent clients are in the process of growing out of their state of dependence, both economic and psychological. Hence, many or even most forms of maladaptive student behaviour may represent exploratory processes in the formation of a realistic self-identity. 'The role of the counsellor,' Pallone (1966) writes, 'is to assist clients in the task of achieving integration of self-experience with self-perception and of opening the self-system to the expanding influence of unfolding self-experience'.

The counsellor facilitates this growth of the client by offering understanding and acceptance. Rogers (1951) states:

> 'In the emotional warmth of the relationship with the therapist, the client begins to experience a feeling of safety as he finds that whatever attitude he expresses is accepted and is understood in almost the same way that he perceives it himself. But the therapist perceives these experiences with a new quality. He perceives the client's self as the client knows it and accepts it; he perceives the contradictory aspects which have been denied to awareness and accepts these too as being part of the client and both of these acceptances have in them the same warmth and respect. Thus it is that the client, experiencing in another an acceptance of both these aspects of himself, can take the same attitude toward himself. He can experience himself as a person having hostile as well as other types of feelings and can experience himself in this way without guilt. He has been enabled to do this because another person has been able to adopt his frame of reference, to perceive with him yet to perceive with acceptance and respect.'

Counselling provides the client with an atmosphere which encourages him to become more open. It modifies the self-concept of the client so that he will arrive at a wholesome self-acceptance. And the importance of self-acceptance is underlined by the previously discussed empirical evidence which suggests that as an individual thinks approvingly of himself he is inclined to think approvingly of others; and if he sees himself in an unfavourable light he is likely to view others unfavourably. Self-knowledge, then, is at the heart of counselling in that the more the client knows about himself the better he can understand and appreciate the behaviour of others. Irrespective of the type of problem, effective counselling is gauged by the extent to which the client is assisted to become aware of the totality of his self-experience, to accept this experience and to expand this self-acceptance in the acceptance of others. Coombs (1949) states that the purpose of therapy is to create a situation in which change of perception of the self is formulated and encouraged. As the client is helped to focus his attention on the meaning that experiences have for him, he is clarifying his perception and concept of himself and his relationship to the people and events around him. Breuer (towards the end of the nineteenth century) observed that when hysterical patients were led encouragingly to talk about themselves and to disclose to an accepting ear feelings which they had repressed at the time of certain traumatic experiences, they seem to achieve, with a new self-awareness and self-acceptance, a diminution or disappearance of their symptoms. Freud, more acutely alive to the nature of repression and its profound unconscious roots, emphasised that neurotic and maladjusted people were reluctant to come to know themselves and to face what was for them the pain of self-discovery. Through the use of the analytic technique and carefully timed interventions, they had to be led to the point in time when they were ready both to see and accept themselves as they really were.

Conclusion

In counselling, the self is both the source of the problem and the source of its alleviation. It is from the client's distorted concept of self that his unhappiness and maladaptive behaviour arises. If, in the counselling relationship, he comes to a more realistic self-perception and self-acceptance, his problem will be solved.

5

Measurement of Core Conditions and Core Outcomes

With a view to giving practical application to the foregoing theories, a study was undertaken using senior level secondary students to measure the core conditions and core outcomes of counselling.

5.1 The Instruments Described

5.1.1 Barrett-Lennard's Relationship Inventory

Since this is an investigation of client-centred counselling, it might seem appropriate to use measures developed by Carl Rogers. However, as already noted, Rogers did not distinguish between unconditionality and level of regard and did not devise measures for these variables. Only Barrett-Lennard's Relationship Inventory measures not merely empathy and congruence but all four core conditions. Consequently this was the main instrument chosen for this investigation.

A basic general postulate of counselling and therapy is that the client's experiences of his therapist's response is the chief basis of therapeutic influence in their relationship (Wolberg 1967). Although it is not supposed that a client's conscious perceptions represent with complete accuracy the way he experiences his therapist, the assumption is that, under suitable conditions, this report is the most direct and reliable evidence of his actual experience. Barrett-Lennard's Relationship Inventory provides such a measure of the client's perception of the therapeutic relationship.

The original version of the Relationship Inventory was designed by Barrett-Lennard (1957) to quantify five theoretically critical dimensions of interpersonal relationship assessed *from the point of view of the client*. These dimensions are:

(a) the counsellor's level of regard for his client,
(b) the unconditionality of this regard,
(c) his congruence in the relationship,
(d) the degree of the counsellor's empathic understanding,
(e) his willingness to be known as he really is by the client.

73

Rogers' (1957) 'Conditions of Therapy' and Brown's (1954) 'Relationship Sort' were used in the development of specific items by Barrett-Lennard. He planned to have separate items for each variable. To eliminate any items for which this was not true, a content validation procedure was carried out. Formal directions and definitions of the variables were given to five judges who were all counsellors of varying levels of experience. The judges classified each item as either a positive or negative indicator of the variable in question, and gave a neutral rating to any item that they regarded as irrelevant or ambiguous. Three items whose rating was inconsistent were eliminated. Three consistently rated items were also eliminated mainly because of duplication of content.

The Inventory was originally administered to 42 clients. An item analysis was then conducted. Barrett-Lennard tabulated and compared the answers given to each item by the 'upper' and 'lower' half of the sample divided in terms of scores on the variable to which the item belonged. One item which had been interpreted in two different ways by client respondents was eliminated as a result of this procedure. In the final set of 85 items, each variable was represented by 16–18 items.

Further analysis of the results revealed that willingness to be known was an aspect or expression of congruence rather than a separate variable in its own right. Hence, in a revision of the Inventory, the willingness to be known dimension was eliminated. The inventory then contained 72 items. Barrett-Lennard and Bills (1975) reworded the Inventory so that it would be suitable for administration to students from grades 7 to 12.

DESCRIPTION
The Relationship Inventory is a 72 item instrument which yields scores on the four interpersonal relationship qualities — level of regard, unconditionality, congruence and empathic understanding. The items were arranged in regularly recurring order. Subjects respond to each item by using a six-point Likert-type scale. Scoring is as follows:

Yes, I feel strongly that it is true: +3
Yes, I feel it is true: +2
Yes, I feel that it is probably true, or more true than untrue: +1
No, I feel that it is probably untrue, or more untrue than true: -1
No, I feel it is not true: -2
No, I feel strongly that it is not true: -3

To score the Relationship Inventory, the ratings of certain items are reversed in value to place them on the same scale. In effect, the ratings for positive items have the same values as those for negative items. When the items have been reversed, the positive and negative totals for each scale are determined by subtracting the smaller value from the larger and affixing the sign of the larger. Since there are 18 items on each of the four scales, scores for each scale can vary from -54 to +54.

RELIABILITY

Four studies were carried out to investigate reliability:

1. Barrett-Lennard (1962) obtained the following split-half reliabilities for the scales (N=42): level of regard .93, empathic understanding .86, congruence .89, and unconditionality .92. All estimates were corrected by the Spearman-Brown formula.

2; Bills (1975) quoted corrected split-half correlations for the scales: level of regard .79, empathic understanding .83, unconditionality of regard .58, congruence .58 and total scale .89. As would be expected because of its greater length, the total scale has a higher reliability than any of the subscales.

3. Snelbecker (1961 and 1967) reports split-half reliability coefficients ranging from .75 to .94 for the four scales in separate assessments from two samples of data provided by observers viewing therapy films. He wished to verify that when the Inventory was adapted for such observers it held up in regard to internal reliability.

4. Hollenbeck (1965) obtained split-half reliabilities ranging from .83 to .95 for the four scales in samples of parent-child relationships reported by college students. Test-retest correlations, over a six-month interval, ranged from .61 to .81 for the four scales.

These figures indicate satisfactory internal reliability of the measures.

VALIDITY

Content Validity:

The procedures used in developing the instrument already discussed (i.e. judges' ratings and item analysis) ensured the content validity of the scales.

Construct Validity:

Research that provides evidence relevant to the validation of the Relationship Inventory includes studies by Thornton (1960), Emmerling (1961), Clark and Culbert (1965), Gross and De Ridder (1966) and Van der Veen (1965).

1. Thornton's (1960) findings indicate that the Relationship Inventory scores from the perceptions of either marriage partner are highly correl-

ated with another kind of carefully developed measure (Burgess and Cottrell 1939) of the adequacy of a marriage relationship.

2. Emmerling (1961) employed a criterion of 'open-mindedness' based on Q-sort data which was designed to distinguish between relatively effective and ineffective teachers on the basis of the degree to which they saw themselves as responsible for solving difficulties and providing remedial action in their work situation. The fact that the pupils of more open teachers did describe them more positively on each of the Relationship Inventory dimensions implies that the measures were sensitive to differences consistent with prediction and theory.

3. Clark and Culbert (1965), Gross and De Ridder (1966) and Van der Veen (1965) investigated associations between measures of functioning based on the Rogers' psychotherapy process scale (Rogers 1967) and the Relationship Inventory dimensions. The positive findings of association between these two theoretically related classes of measures provide further endorsement of the measuring procedures.

Research applications of the Relationship Inventory in many languages run to several hundred studies as a cursory examination of recent bibliographies by Barrett-Lennard (1972) and by Barrett-Lennard and Bergersen (1975) reveals. These studies report high reliability and validity.

5.1.2 Bills' High School Index of Adjustment and Values

A review of the literature led to the decision to use Bills' High School Index of Adjustment and Values to measure self-concept, self-acceptance and ideal self. Although Rogers (1961) frequently used the Q-sort technique of Stephenson, Wylie (1961) has raised serious doubts concerning the construct validity of this kind of instrument as a measure of self-concept. She noted that the subject's arrangement of items along the 'like me' continuum may indicate chiefly his general level of self-regard. The items may sample widely or narrowly the total possible range of levels of self-regard and the total population of characteristics about which self-regard may vary. Accordingly, the subject's sort may be influenced to a greater or lesser degree by his general level of self-regard. Mowrer (1953), Cronbach (1953) and Cronbach and Glaser (1953) state that the introduction of forced sorting restricts the range of individual differences in general self-regard which can be obtained from the self-sort alone.

Of Bills' Index of Adjustment and Values, Wylie (1961) states: 'Much more information is available on the norms, reliability and validity of this instrument than on any other measure of the self-concept included in this survey.' She claims further that 'such an instrument is superior to a Q-sorting technique'. The High School version evolved from an adult version of an Index of Adjustment and Values (IAV) designed by Bills, Vance and Mc Lean (1951).

In the development of the instrument, a sample of 124 words was taken from Allport and Odbert's 1936 list of 17,953 traits. In selecting these words an effort was made to choose items which occur frequently in client-centred interviews and which seemed to present clear examples of self- concept definitions. After an item analysis of the results of a three-week test- retest study involving 44 college students, items of low reliability were eliminated. The IAV then contained 49 words.

In 1959, three further forms, the Elementary School Form, the Junior High School Form and the High School Form were published. In the development of the High School IAV, the method employed was classroom visitation where several questions were asked, e.g., 'What do you like most about yourself?'; 'What do you like least about yourself?'; 'Give me the one word you think of when I say "mother", "father", "teacher" and "principal".'

From the trait words thus compiled three lists were selected for initial trial. These contained words which expressed the most frequently given personal attributes. On the basis of item analyses, these trial forms were later revised for content. Nine of the trait words are identical on the adult and high school version of the IAV.

DESCRIPTION
The High School IAV consists of 37 words arranged in a vertical list with three blank columns after each word. Column 1 samples the concept of self. The subjects are asked to indicate in this column, by the use of a five point scale, the extent to which these words apply to them. A score of 1 indicates seldom, 2 indicates occasionally, 3 indicates about half the time, 4 indicates a good deal of the time and 5 indicates most of the time.

Column 2 measures acceptance of self. The subjects are instructed to give a rating which would tell how they feel about themselves as described in the first column. The ratings are as follows:

(1) I very much dislike being as I am in this respect.
(2) I dislike being as I am in this respect.
(3) I neither dislike nor like being as I am in this respect.
(4) I like being as I am in this respect.
(5) I very much like being as I am in this respect.

Column 3 samples the concept of the ideal self. The subjects are instructed to use each of the words to complete the sentence 'I would like to be a (an) – person', and to indicate in the third column how much of the time they would like this trait to be characteristic of them. The same rating system is used as in column 1.

The 'others' form of the High School IAV is similar to the 'self' form except that the subject is asked to complete the index as he thinks another person would complete it for himself.

Reliability
Split-half reliabilities, corrected for the full length of each scale by the Spearman-Brown formula, were obtained by Bills (1975). All coefficients were found to be significant at less than the .01 level of confidence.

VALIDITY
Content Validity
In the development of the High School IAV, all the words used were obtained from children at senior high school. These are words which children use to describe themselves and other people. The list of words was revised as a result of item analysis.

5.1.3 Berger's Acceptance of Self and Others Scale
The last core outcome investigated was acceptance of others. A scrutiny of the literature showed that Berger's Acceptance of Self and Others Scale was highly suited to this purpose. Shaw and Wright (1967), in their review say of this scale that 'it is the most carefully developed scale that we found. Evidence of validity is more extensive than for most scales.'

Berger (1952) used an abridged and slightly modified version of Sheerer's (1949) definitions in the development of the scale. According to him, the self-accepting person:

(1) assumes responsibility for and accepts the consequences of his own behaviour;
(2) accepts praise or criticism from others gracefully;
(3) does not attempt to deny or distort any feelings, motives, limitations, abilities or favourable qualities which he sees in himself, but rather accepts all without condemnation;
(4) relies primarily upon internalized values and standards rather than on external pressure as a guide for his behaviour;
(5) has faith in his capacity to cope with life;
(6) considers himself as a person of worth on an equal plane with other persons;
(7) does not expect others to reject him whether he gives them any reason to or not;

    (8) does not regard himself as totally different from others, or generally abnormal in his reactions;

    (9) is not shy or self-conscious.

Sheerer (1949) lists seven characteristics of the person who accepts others.

    (1) He does not reject, hate or pass judgement on other persons when their behaviour or standards seem to him to be contradictory to his own.

    (2) He does not attempt to dominate others.

    (3) He does not attempt to assume responsibility for others.

    (4) He does not deny the worth of others or their equality with him as persons. This does not imply equality in regard to specific achievements. He feels neither above nor below the people he meets.

    (5) He takes an active interest in others and shows a desire to create mutually satisfactory relationships with them.

    (6) He shows a desire to serve others.

    (7) In attempting to advance his own welfare, he is careful not to infringe on the rights of others.

Using the various elements that make up the definitions as a guide, statements about the self and others were selected or constructed so that they expressed these elements. The preliminary scales consisted of 47 statements on self-acceptance and 40 on acceptance of others. Items from both scales were mixed together on the same form.

The preliminary scales were tested on 200 university students consisting of individuals with widely different socio-economic backgrounds and vocational interests.

Berger then carried out an item analysis. Those subjects whose total scores were in the top 25 per cent were compared on each item with those whose total scores were in the bottom 25 per cent. There were 50 in each criterion group. The difference between the mean scores of the criterion groups was computed for each item. This difference was used as an index of the discriminating power of the item. The standard error of the difference of the quartile means did not exceed .30 for any item. All the items used in the final form of the scales with three exceptions had critical ratios of 3.00 or more. These three exceptions had critical ratios close to 2.00. The final selection of items was made on the basis of their appropriateness and their discriminating ability. Thirty-six items were selected for the self-acceptance scale and twenty-eight for the acceptance of others scale. Each scale of the test was divided into matched halves. Items of both scales were then mixed together in each half at random.

DESCRIPTION

A modified Likert type scale is used for the 36 items. The subject responds to each item by scoring 1 for 'not at all true of myself', 2 for 'slightly true of myself', 3 for 'about half true of myself', 4 for 'mostly true of myself', and 5 for 'true of myself'. The direction of the scoring is reversed for negatively worded items. After this adjustment has been made, the acceptance of self score is computed by summing the item scores for all items on that scale. Similarly, the acceptance of others score is obtained by summing item scores for that scale. A high score indicates a favourable attitude toward self or others.

Reliability

Split-half reliabilities were obtained for five groups ranging in size from 18 to 183 (Berger 1952). These were reported to be .894 or better for the acceptance scale for four of the groups and .746 for the remaining fifth group. All estimates were corrected by the Spearman Brown formula.

Validity

Berger (1952) asked one group of subjects (N=20) to write freely about their attitudes towards themselves, and a second group (N=20) to write about their attitudes towards others. These essays were then rated by four judges and the mean ratings correlated with the corresponding scale scores. The Pearson product-moment correlation between scores and ratings was .897 for self-acceptance and .727 for acceptance of others. Both of these correlations were statistically significant. The average of the inter-correlations among judges' rating was .869 for self-acceptance and .769 for acceptance of others.

A group of stutterers was compared with a group of non-stutterers, matched for age and sex. As expected, the group of stutterers scored lower on self-acceptance. For the acceptance of others scale, a group of prisoners was compared with a group of college students matched for age, sex and race. Again, as expected, prisoners scored lower on the acceptance of others scale than the students, the difference being significant at the .02 level. The prisoners also scored lower on the self-acceptance scale, the difference being significant at the .01 level.

5.2 The Instruments Applied

The three instruments already described, namely Bills' Index of Adjustment and Values, Barrett-Lennard's Relationship Inventory and Berger's Self-acceptance/Acceptance of Others Scale were used to measure the following variables:

client self-concept,
client self-acceptance,
client self-ideal,
client estimate of his ability to accept other people,
client estimate of counsellor's self-concept,
client estimate of counsellor's self-ideal,
client estimate of counsellor's level of regard,
client estimate of counsellor's empathy,
client estimate of counsellor's unconditionality of attitude,
client estimate of counsellor's congruence.

Initially 123 students (Baseline) participated in the investigation. Sixty-seven of this group continued with counselling to the Intermediate stage. Forty-one of these sixty seven students remained until the Final stage. The table which follows represents this diagrammatically.

TABLE 1

Baseline Stage	Intermediate Stage	Final Stage
G_{abc} (N = 123)	G_{bc} (N = 67)	G_c (N = 41)
G_a (N = 56)		
G_b (N = 26)	G_b (N = 26)	
G_c (N = 41)	G_c (N = 41)	G_c (N = 41)

The Baseline group G_{abc} comprised all three sub-groups who participated in the study i.e. subjects who attended at least two counselling sessions. G_a (N = 56) refers to those subjects who terminated counselling after being tested once at the end of the second session. G_b (N = 26) refers to the number of students who terminated counselling after being tested twice. G_c (N = 41) comprises those students who persevered with counselling and were tested three times. G_{bc} is, therefore, composed of 2 sub-groups, twenty-six of whom (G_b) terminated counselling at the Intermediate stage, and forty-one (G_c) who persevered to the final stage and were tested three times.

5.2.1 Pilot and Main Studies

Pilot Study

In view of possible cross-cultural effects, it was considered desirable to administer the tests in a pilot study to confirm their appropriateness for use with Irish students and to find the average length of time needed for completion. The questionnaires were administered in a secondary school which was *not* included in the sample selected for the main study. Seventeen students were tested.

This preliminary investigation revealed that the tests posed no difficulty apart from a query from one student as to the meaning of 'democratic' in Bills' High School Index of Adjustment and Values. The average time for completion was fifty minutes.

Main Study

The main study was carried out in 1977. The subjects were fifth year and sixth year students in secondary schools. A sample of approximately one hundred subjects was sought in an effort to provide a broadly based set of observations. It was estimated that guidance counsellors dealt with an average of ten counselling cases per year from the senior cycle. To allow for low response rates in some cases, twelve counsellors were asked to participate in the research in order to obtain the target sample of one hundred subjects.

Since the relationship of the guidance counsellor to the students was considered to be an important factor, this was taken into consideration in the determination of sample size. From personal contact and discussion on a monthly basis during the previous three years with various guidance counsellors, it was clear that while some counsellors spent a considerable amount of time with their clients, others devoted very little time to them. Hence the invitation to participate was restricted to twelve of the former. Of these, ten accepted. Of the two who did not, one did not have the time necessary for counselling due to a heavy workload, the other cited the reluctance of her school principal to allow research in counselling in the school. These two counsellors were replaced by two others who had just qualified in guidance counselling and who regarded counselling as one of their main tasks.

Of the twelve counsellors, three were men and nine were women, which reflected the general ratio in the register of the Institute of Guidance Counsellors of Ireland. They were all based in second level schools in Cork city and county. Their years of experience prior to the study varied from none to six years. Since qualified guidance counsellors have only been in second level education since 1968, this covered almost the entire spectrum in terms of length of experience.

The number of clients was one hundred and twenty-three. Forty-four were males and seventy- nine were females. Forty- two were fifth year and seventy-nine were sixth year students. Two did not fill in this particular item of information on the questionnaire. In terms of geographical location, the subjects came from seven urban and from four rural schools. One counsellor had no client for the entire year. Pupils in her school came to her solely for vocational guidance. It is worthy of mention that this counsellor was just beginning a career in counselling. Of the eleven schools that participated, five had female students only, three had male students only, three were co-educational schools. Six of the schools had day pupils only, whereas the remaining five had both day and boarding pupils.

Subjects were selected according to the following criteria:

(I)   'voluntary' clients who sought counselling;

(II) non-psychiatric cases, in the sense that they were not currently under psychiatric treatment;

(III) students who had not approached the counsellor previously with a 'counselling' problem. (This was to allow for control of the 'core conditions').

The counsellors asked the clients to complete Bills' Index of Adjustment and Values, Barrett-Lennard's Relationship Inventory and Berger's Self-Acceptance/Acceptance of Others Scale after the second counselling session. The tests were repeated after each subsequent session.

One aspect of the validity problem requires comment here, namely, whether the responses of the students were a true reflection of their conscious experience and their estimation of the counsellors or whether they indicated what the clients felt would please the counsellors. To obviate this possibility, it was emphasised that the counsellor would not see or have access to the answers. It was left to the students themselves to mail the replies to University College Cork. Clients were also reminded that the value of their contribution for research purposes depended on the extent to which it represented their actual perceptions of the counselling relationship.

5.2.2 Data Processing and Analysis

From Barrett-Lennard's Relationship Inventory, scores were obtained for level of regard, empathy, unconditionality of attitude and congruence. From Bills' High School Index of Adjustment and Values, scores were obtained for self-concept, self-acceptance and self-ideal. From Berger's scale, scores were obtained for self-acceptance and acceptance of others. Having scored each form, the data was transferred onto cards for the computer as follows:

Fig. 1

Subject's acceptance of others	55-57	☐
Subject's self-acceptance (Berger's Scale)	52-54	☐
	50-51	☐
Subject's estimate of the counsellor's congruence	47-49	☐
Subject's estimate of the counsellor's unconditionality	44-46	☐
Subject's estimate of the counsellor's empathy	41-43	☐
Subject's estimate of the counsellor's level of regard	38-40	☐
	36-37	☐
Client's estimate of counsellor's self-ideal	33-35	☐
Client's estimate of counsellor's self-acceptance	30-32	☐
Client's estimate of counsellor's self-concept	27-29	☐
	25-26	☐
Subject's self-ideal	22-24	☐
Subject's self-acceptance (Bills' Scale)	19-21	☐
Subject's self-concept	16-18	☐
	14-15	☐
Male or Female subject	12	☐
Fifth year or sixth year subject	13	
Whether the client is a current or former pupil of the counsellor	10-11	☐
Identity of counsellor	8-9	☐
	6-7	☐
Test identification (first, second or third)	5	☐
The number of times the scales were completed	4	☐
The subject's identity number	1-3	☐

Data Analysis

The computer was programmed to provide the means and standard deviations for each of the variables at the Baseline, Intermediate and Final stages of counselling. One way analyses of variance for independent groups were performed to test for significant differences between each of the three groups at the Baseline stage on each of the variables.

When an overall significant 'F' was obtained, post-hoc comparisons were carried out using Scheffe's test. A critical ratio test for identical groups was applied to the scores of the Gbc groups at the Baseline and Intermediate stages. A 't' test for independent groups was performed to ascertain significant differences between the scores of the Gb and Gc groups at the Intermediate stage on each of the variables.

Finally, one way analyses of variance for repeated measures were performed to test for significant differences between the scores of the Gc group at the Baseline, Intermediate and Final stages of counselling. When an overall significant 'F' was obtained, post-hoc comparisons were carried out using the Duncan Multiple Range test (1967).

FINDINGS

Analyses of variance confirmed that those who terminated counselling at the Baseline, Intermediate and Final stages did not differ on any of the variables at the Baseline stage except on acceptance of others. Forty-five per cent of all clients did not continue to the Intermediate stage of counselling. For the sixty-seven individuals who remained in counselling, a significant increase occurred on the client's self-concept. They also increased on self-acceptance as measured by both Bills and Berger and on the client's perception of the counsellor's level of empathy. Of these sixty-seven, twenty-six continued only to the Intermediate stage, forty-one to the Final stage. However, while the group of twenty-six showed a significant increase on both the Bills and Berger self-acceptance scales, the group of forty-one showed an increase on the Bills' self-acceptance scale between the Baseline and Intermediate stages and on Berger's Self-acceptance and Acceptance of Others scale between the Intermediate and Final Stages. At the Intermediate stage, there were no measurable differences between those who continued and those who terminated.

Conclusions

The results of the research indicated that:

(1) A sizeable number of the clients (45%) terminate counselling after the initial stage.
(2) Of the counsellor-offered conditions in counselling, namely, empathy, congruence, level of regard and unconditionality, empathy is the most significant.
(3) Empathy is established early in the ralationship or not at all.
(4) A significant increase in self-acceptance would appear to be the criterion for successful counselling.

A notable feature of the study, then, was the large number of clients who terminated counselling in the initial stages.

'TERMINATOR' CHARACTERISTICS

The 'terminator' emerged as someone unable to accept offered help from either formal or informal sources. When faced with the counsellor, his negative attitude towards people in general, as well as his inability to share his feelings and experiences, seem to prevent him from continuing long in counselling.

Additional hypotheses on the nature and causes of termination may be (a) the unsuitability of a particular method for a percentage of any group of clients and (b) the effects of cultural bias against counselling. The seeking of help from a counsellor by the client may have connotations akin to visiting a psychiatrist, the social stigma of which has been discussed by Moran (1976) and Orford (1976). Alternatively, it may be that the client has a confused idea of what to expect of the counsellor. He may expect the provision of immediate help and, when he does not find this, he may leave counselling. Hence, counsellors should be aware of the necessity of explaining to the client the nature of counselling, because he may expect to be the passive recipient of help rather than his own therapeutic agent. As Dunne (1978) points out, while the counsellor may be the facilitator, the client is the agent of his own cure to a significant extent. It may be that some or all of these elements interact to determine whether a client is a terminator or not. These hypotheses require thorough investigation.

It would seem to be important to make a real effort to comprehend the problem of terminators since the consistently high number reported suggests that counselling, not infrequently, can fail to help clients in their need.

The question arises whether 'spontaneous remission' accounted for this drop-out rate. Research indicates that spontaneous remission would seem to be due (a) to informal therapeutic influences (Frank 1961) and (b) to the personal characteristics of the terminators (Grummon 1954). Frank (1961) found that many disturbed persons who receive no formal psychotherapy, sought and obtained help from various other sources, such as friends, clergymen, physicians and teachers. They sought and obtained a relationship that provided the core therapeutic factors in their lives. Grummon (1954) analyzed the test results of a two month no-therapy period for a control group of patients. From his investigation it emerged that eight of the twenty-three clients in the group chose not to enter therapy while the other fifteen did. Those who chose not to enter therapy showed significant improvement in many of the measures during the non-therapy period. The continuing group, however, showed no improvement at all during the waiting period. This seems to imply that people who remain in therapy are self-selected and do not improve without therapy.

The suggestion from this is that 'spontaneous remission' did not account for the drop-out rate in the present study since the terminators scored significantly lower on acceptance of others than those who remained in counselling. This seems to indicate that the members of this group would not be open to informal therapeutic influences. The drop-out time span was significantly shorter than any of the control periods in the spontaneous remission studies reported in the literature (Kurland 1965, Rosenthal and Frank 1956) thus making it unlikely that significant personal changes could have occurred in these clients.

EMPATHY

Of the four counselling conditions investigated, perceived empathy was clearly the most significant. It was the only one of the four elements that improved significantly in the counselling process. This improvement took place between the Baseline and Intermediate stages. This concurs with the findings of Truax (1963) and supports Tausch's conclusion that the degree of empathy which exists or will exist in the counselling relationship can be detected and measured at an early stage therein. The other three conditions, congruence, unconditionality and level of regard, while continuing to be present, did not increase in the perception of the client.

Munroe (1955) has attested to the importance of empathy in the counselling relationship, and Wolberg (1967) stated: 'Perhaps the most important characteristic of the good therapist is his capacity for empathy', a viewpoint amply confirmed in the present research. This is not surprising when we consider that, for the client, empathy means that someone understands him just as he is. Through the experience of this understanding he is enabled to discuss himself more freely and fully. He can examine himself more closely without being distracted by having to remain on guard against the criticism he might usually fear in a non-therapeutic atmosphere. His attention is not divided and he can actually examine the specific aspects of his self-concept which are causing difficulty. Eventually he is able to see himself in a more positive manner which, in turn, leads to greater self-acceptance. This has been emphasized by Raimy (1948) for whom, in formal psychotherapeutic situations, the essential structural relationships within the client's self-concept are altered, with resultant increased feelings of comfort and effectiveness.

In this study, client-perceived measures of empathy were employed. Distinct phases of such empathy have been enumerated by Barrett-Lennard (1976). These are:

(1) The 'inner' process of empathic listening, resonation and personal understanding.
(2) Communicated or expressed empathic understanding on the part of the counsellor.
(3) Received empathy, or empathy as experienced by the client.

Depending upon which step or phase in this sequence is being tapped different measures are appropriate. Kurtz and Grummon (1972) used an indirect approach to assessing phase (1) above. They asked therapists to predict how their clients would describe themselves on a series of self-descriptive personality items.

Counsellor-communicated empathy (phase 2 above) has been measured by the Truax-Carkhuff rating scales in which an independent judge rates the level of therapist empathy in an interview from an audio tape-recording of it. Samples of three to five minutes are excerpted from the recording.

The Barrett-Lennard Relationship Inventory focuses on what the client experiences, upon his perceptions of being understood and accepted. Barrett-Lennard believes that empathy, to be effective, should be communicated to and be perceived by the client. A low score on the Relationship Inventory, however, does not necessarily imply the absence of empathy but rather its non-perception by the client and its corresponding ineffectiveness. This measure of Barrett-Lennard's seems to be one of the most relevant and reliable in relation to counselling and therapy.

It would then seem appropriate that future research should concentrate on methods and techniques for the early establishment of perceived empathy. It would also help to identify what particular personality types are more suited as empathic counsellors. It is desirable to discover whether empathy can be increased with training and, if so, what form the training should take. It should also ascertain to what extent non-verbal behaviour affects the level of empathy in the relationship. It would also appear worthwhile to study and, perhaps, validate the three phases of empathy described by Barrett-Lennard. The research of Truax (1961, 1962) and Van der Veen (1965), which aimed at determining whether the onus of creating an adequate level of empathy in a given therapeutic situation is a matter for the counsellor or the client, becomes largely irrelevant if Barrett-Lennard's conclusions are correct.

SELF–ACCEPTANCE

An examination of the Bills scale in regard to self-aceeptance shows that it is based mainly on social interaction. The client may complete it from two different perspectives. He can take either his own perception of himself or his perception of how others view him. The Berger scale, however, appears much more probing of psychodynamic functioning. It requires that the client complete it as he sees himself irrespective of how others see him. It demands that he face his inner conflicts and stresses and examine himself much more sharply than in the Bills scale.

If we accept this basis for differentiation between the two scales, it would seem reasonable that the client should increase on self-acceptance as measured by Berger before he is ready to terminate counselling. The result would also seem to have both a diagnostic and research use in that it suggests that the Berger scale could be used to monitor the progress and effectiveness of counselling.

With regard to the dimensions of self-acceptance and acceptance of others, the present study provided data both for those clients who continued and those clients who terminated counselling, as well as indications concerning the measuring instruments employed.

The twenty-six clients who left counselling at the Intermediate stage increased significantly on both the Bills and Berger self-acceptance scales. The forty-one clients who remained until the Final stage showed an increase on Bills' self-acceptance scale between the Baseline and Intermediate stages and on Berger's self-acceptance and acceptance of others scales between the Intermediate and Final stages. The results agree, with some qualification, with those of other researchers. The study of Feifel and Eels (1963) noted that the change most frequently occurring as a result of therapy, as evaluated by clients, is a more realistic evaluation of self. Similarly Raimy (1948), Sheerer (1949) and Stock (1949) concluded from their investigation that, in successful client-centred counselling, there was a movement from negative to positive feelings about the self. These authors also mentioned that acceptance of self was usually accompanied by acceptance of others.

The results of the present study suggest some qualifications with regard to these conclusions. From the different pattern of reactions of the two groups of twenty-six and forty-one clients, it would seem that self-acceptance and acceptance of others need not occur simultaneously. If psychological well-being is a balance between the amount of attention given to oneself, to other individuals and to one's environment, then those clients who persevered to the Final stage possibly achieved greater personal equilibrium.

Bibliography

Adler, A. *The practice and theory of individual psychology.* New York: Harcourt Brace Press, 1924.

Adler, A. *The neurotic constitution.* New York: Dodd Mead Press, 1926.

Allen, P. *Psychotherapy with children.* New York: Norton Press, 1942.

Allport, G. W. 'Scientific models and human morals'. *Psychological Review,* 54, 182-192, 1946.

Allport, G. W. *Personality: A Psychological Interpretation.* London: Constable Co., 1949.

Allport, G. W. *The Nature of Personality. Selected Papers.* Cambridge: Addison-Wesley, 1950.

Allport, G. W. *Becoming: Basic Considerations for a Psychology of Personality.* New Haven: Yale University Press, 1955.

Arnold, M. and Gasson, J. *The Human Person, An Approach to an Integral Theory of Personality.* New York: Ronald Press, 1954.

Aspy, D. *Toward a Technology for Humanizing Education.* Illinois: Champaign Research Press, 1972.

Auld, F. and Myers, J. K. 'Contribution to a theory for selecting psychotherapy patients'. *Journal of Clinical Psychology,* 10, 56-60, 1954.

Aylwin, S. *On being permeable.* Paper given at Philosophical Seminar, Spring Meeting, U.C. Cork, 1979.

Azrin, N. H. and Holz, W. C. 'Punishment'. Cited in Honig, W. K. (ed.) *Operant Behaviour: areas of research and application.* New York: Appleton Press, 1966.

Backman, C. W. and Secord, P. F. 'The effect of perceived liking on interpersonal attractin'. *Human Relations.* 12, 379-384, 1959.

Baker, B. O. and Black, J. 'Predictability and predictive ability as functions of personality style and self-criticality', *American Psychologist,* 10, 346, 1955.

Barrett-Lennard, G. T. 'Dimensions of perceived therapist response related to therapeutic change.' Unpublished Ph.D. thesis. University of Chicago, 1959.

Barrett-Lennard, G. T. 'Dimensions of therapist response as causal factors in therapeutic change'. *Psychological Monographs,* 76, 562, 1962.

Barrett-Lennard, G. T. *Resource Bibliography of reported studies using the Relationship Inventory.* University of Waterloo Press, 1972.

Barrett-Lennard, 'Empathy in Human Relationships: significance, nature and measurement'. *Australian Psychologist,* 11, 2, 173-184, 1976.

Barrett-Lennard, G. T. and Bergersen, S. G. *Recent Bibliography of reported studies using the Relationship Inventory.* University of Waterloo, 1972.

Baum, O. E., Felzer, S., D'Zmura, T. and Shumaker, E. 'Psychotherapy Dropouts and Lower Socioeconomic patients'. *American Journal of Orthopsychiatry,* 36, 629-635, 1966.

Bell, G. B. and Hall, H. E. 'The Relationship between Leadership and Empathy'. *Journal of Abnormal and Social Psychology,* 49, 156-157, 1954.

Berger, E. M. 'The relation between expressed acceptance of self and expressed acceptance of others'. *Journal of Abnormal and Social Psychology,* 47, 770-780, 1952.

Bergin, A. E. and Jasper, L. G. 'Correlates of empathy in psychotherapy: a replication'. *Journal of Abnormal Psychology,* 14, 345-349. 1969.

Bergin, A. E. and Solomon, S. 'Personality and performance correlates of empathic understanding in psychotherapy'. Cited in Tomlinson, T. and Hart, J. (eds). *New directions in client-centred therapy.* Boston: Houghton-Mifflin Press, 1970.

Bills, R. E. *A System for Measuring Affectivity.* University of Alabama Press, 1975.

Bills, R.E., Vance, E. L. and McLean, O. S. 'An index of adjustment and values'. *Journal of Consulting Psychology,* 15, 257-261, 1951.

Blocksma, D. D. 'An experiment in counsellor learning'. Unpublished Ph.D. thesis, University of Chicago, 1951.

Brownfain, J. J. 'Stability of self-concept as a dimension of personality'. *Journal of Abnormal and Social Psychology,* 47, 597-606, 1952.

Brown, O. H. 'An investigation of therapeutic relationships in client-centred psychotherapy'. Unpublished Ph.D. thesis, University of Chicago, 1954.

Breuer, J. and Freud, S. *Studies in Hysteria. Translated by Brill, A. A.* New York: Nervous and Mental Disorders Publishing Company, 1936.

Braatov, T. *Fundamentals of psychoanalytic technique.* New York: Wiley Press, 1954.

Burgess, E. W. and Cottrell, L. S. *Predicting success or failure.* New York: Prentice-Hall Press, 1939.

Butler, J. M. 'Addressing psychotherapeutic protocols with context coefficients'. *Journal of Clinical Psychology*, 9, 199-202, 1952.

Butler, J. M. and Haigh, G. V. 'Changes in the relation between self-concept and ideal-self.' In Roger, C. R. and Dymond, R. F. *Psychotherapy and Personality Change.* Chicago: University of Chicago Press, 1954.

Cahoon, R. A. 'Some counsellor attitudes and characteristics related to the counselling relationship'. Unpublished Ph.D. thesis, Ohio State University, 1962.

Campbell, R. J. 'The development and validation of a multiple-choice scale to measure affective sensitivity (empathy)'. Unpublished doctoral thesis. Michigan State University, Ann Arbor, Michigan, 1967.

Campbell, R. J., Kagan, N., and Krathwohl, D. 'The Development and Validation of a Scale to Measure Affective Sensitivity (Empathy)'. *Journal of Counselling Psychology*, 18, No. 5, 407-412, 1971.

Carkhuff, R. R. 'Critical variables in effective counsellor training'. *Journal of Counselling Psychology*, 16, 238-245, 1969.

Carkhuff, R. R. *Helping and Human Relations* Vol. I. New York: Holt, Rinehart and Winston Press, 1969.

Carkhuff, R. R. *The art of helping.* Massachusetts: Carkhuff Associates, 1972.

Carkhuff, R. R. and Berenson, B. G. *Beyond counselling and therapy.* New York: Holt, Rinehart and Winston Press, 1967.

Cartwright, R. and Lerner, B. 'Empathy, need to change and improvement with psychotherapy'. *Journal of Consulting Psychology*, 1963, 27, 138-144.

Chapman, J. L. 'The development and validation of a scale to measure empathy'. Unpublished doctoral thesis. Michigan State University. Ann Arbor, Michigan, 1966.

Clark, J. V. and Culbert, S. A. 'Mutually therapeutic perception and awareness in a T group'. *Journal of Applied Behavioural Science*, 1 (2), 180-194, 1965.

Clifford, E. and Clifford, M. 'Self-concepts before and after survival training'. *British Journal of Social and Clinical Psychology,* 6, 241-248, 1967.

Cohen, A. R. 'Some implications of self-esteem for social influence'. In Hovland, C.I. and Janis, I.L. (eds). *Personality and persuasibility.* New Haven: Yale University Press, 1959.

Cohen, A. R. 'Experimental Effects of Ego-defense Preference in Interpersonal Relations'. *Journal of Abnormal and Social Psychology,* 52, 19-27, 1956.

Coombs, A. W. 'A coordinated research in psychotherapy'. *Journal of Consulting Psychology,* 13, 149-220, 1949.

Conn, L. 'Instigation to aggression, emotional arousal and defensive emulation'. Unpublished Master's thesis, Ohio State University, 1962.

Cooley, C. M. *Human nature and the social order.* New York: Scribner's Press, 1902.

Coopersmith, S. *The antecedents of self-esteem.* San Francisco: Freeman, 1967.

Cronbach, L. J. 'Correlations between persons as a research tool'. In Mowrer, O. H. (ed). *Psychotherapy: theory and research.* New York: Ronald Press, 1953.

Cronbach, L. J. and Glaser, G. C. 'Assessing similarity between profiles'. *Psychological Bulletin,* 50, 456-473, 1953.

Curran, A. 'The problem of assessing psychiatric treatment'. *Lancet,* 2: 1005, 1937.

Dempsey, P. J. R. *The Self: Some Aspects of a significant Concept.* Paper read at Psychological Society of Ireland Conference, Cork, 1975.

Dengrove, E. 'Why patients discontinue treatment in a mental hygiene clinic'. *American Journal of Psychotherapy,* 4, 457-472, 1950.

Denker, P. G. 'Result of treatment of psychoneuroses by the general practitioner—a follow-up study of 500 cases treated'. *New York: State Journal of Medicine,* 46, 2164, 1946.

Deutsch, F. 'Analytic posturology'. *Psychoanalytic Quarterly,* 21, 196-214, 1951.

Deutsch, M. and Solomon, L. 'Reactions to evaluation by others as influenced by self-evaluations'. *Sociometry,* 22, 93-112, 1959.

Diggory, J. C. *Self-evaluation: Concepts and Studies.* New York: Wiley Press, 1955 (1st Ed.), 1966 (2nd Ed.)

Dimmitt, J. S. 'The congruence of past and ideal self-concepts in the aging male'. *Dissertation abstracts,* 20, 2933, 1959.

Dittes, J. E. 'Attractiveness of a group as a function of self-esteem and acceptance by the group'. *Journal of Abnormal and Social Psychology,* 59, 77-82, 1959.

Dittes, J. E. and Kelly, H. H. 'Effects of different conditions of acceptance upon conformity to group norms'. *Journal of Abnormal and Social Psychology,* 53, 100-107, 1956.

Dollard, J. and Miller , N. *Personality and psychotherapy.* New York: McGraw-Hill, 1950.

Duncan, D. B. 'Multiple range tests for correlated and heteroscedastic means'. *Biometrics,* 13, 164-176, 1967.

Dunne, E. 'The Role of Rehabilitation in the treatment of Psychiatric Patients'. *Galway Medical Annual. Connacht Tribune Press,* 1978.

Dymond, R. F. 'A preliminary investigation of the relation of insight and empathy'. *Journal of Consulting Psychology,* 12, 228-233, 1948.

Dymond, R. F. 'The measurement of empathic ability'. *Journal of Consulting Psychology,* 13, 127-133, 1949.

Dymond, R. F. 'Personality and Empathy'. *Journal of Consulting and Clinical Psychology,* 14, 345-349, 1950.

Dymond, R. F. *Predictive accuracy and the effectiveness of psychotherapy.* Paper read at the American Psychological Association, Washington, D.C., 1952.

Dymond, R. F., Hughes, A. S. and Raabe, V. L. 'Measurable changes in empathy with age'. *Journal of Consulting Psychology,* 16, 202-206, 1952.

Egan, G. *The Skilled Helper.* Monterey, California: Brooks/Cole, 1975.

Eisenberg, S. and Delaney, D. *The Counselling Process.* Chicago: Rand McNally Company, 1976.

Eldred, S. H., Hamburg, D. A., Inwood, E. R., Saltzman, L., Myersburg, H. A. and Goodrich, G. 'A procedure for the systematic analysis of psychotherapeutic interviews'. *Psychiatry,* 17, 337-345, 1954.

Emmerling, F. C. 'A study of the relationship between personality characteristics of classroom teachers'. Unpublished Ph.D. thesis, Auburn University, 1961.

Engel, M. 'The stability of the self-concept in adolescence'. *Journal of Abnormal and Social Psychology,* 58, 211-215, 1959.

Eysenck, H. J. 'The effects of psychotherapy: an evaluation'. *Journal of Consulting Psychology*, 16, 319-324, 1952.

Feifel, H. and Eels, J. 'Patient and therapist assess the same psychotherapy'. *Journal of Counselling Psychology*, 27, 310-318, 1963.

Festinger, L. 'A theory of social comparison processes'. *Human Relations*, 7, 117-140, 1954.

Fey, W. F. 'Acceptance by others and its relation to acceptance of self and others'. *Journal of Abnormal and Social Psychology*, 50, 274-276, 1955.

Fieldler, F. E. 'The concept of an ideal therapeutic relationship'. *Journal of Consulting Psychology*, 14, 239-245, 1950.

Fleege, U. *Self Revelation of the Adolescent Boy*. Milwaukee: Bruce Press, 1945.

Frank, J. D. *Persuasion and Healing: A Comparative Study of Psychotherapy*. Baltimore: John Hopkins Press, 1961.

Frank, J. D., Gliedman, L. H., Imber, S. D., Nash, E. H. and Stone, A. R. 'Why patients leave psychotherapy'. *A.M.A. Archives of Neurological Psychiatry*, 77, 283-299, 1957.

Frank, V. *Psychotherapy and Existentialism* London: Pelican, 1973.

Freud, S. *Group Psychology and Analysis of the Ego*. London: Hogarth Press, 1921.

Freud, S. *The Ego and the Id*. London: Hogarth Press, 1923.

Freud, S. *Further recommendations in the technique of psychoanalysis. Collected papers*. Vol. 2, London: Hogarth Press, 1949.

Freud, S. *Beyond the Pleasure Principle*. London: Hogarth Press, 1955.

Fromm, E. 'Selfishness and Self-love. *Psychiatry*, 2, 507-523, 1939.

Fromm-Reichman, F. 'Remarks on the philosophy of mental disorders'. In P. Mullahy (ed). *A study of interpersonal relations*. New York: Hermitage Press, 1949.

Fromm-Reichman, F. *The principles of intensive psychotherapy*. Chicago: University of Chicago Press, 1950.

Gallagher, J. J. *Group report of a programme of research in psychotherapy*. State College Pennsylvania, 1953.

Garduk, E. L. and Haggard, E. 'Immediate effects on patients of psychoanalytic interpretation'. *Psychological Issues* 7 (4), 1972.

Gendlin, E. T. *Experiencing and the Creation of Meaning*. New York: Free Press, 1962.

Gordon, K. 'A device for demonstrating empathy'. *Journal of Experimental Psychology*, 17, 892-893, 1934.

Griffin, E., Smithson, J., Ellenburgh, K., Gunn, D. and Statts, T. 'A study of the relationship of teacher openness to students perceptions of classroom life, their relationships with their teachers and themselves'. Unpublished paper, University of Alabama, 1972.

Gross, F. and De Ridder, L. M. 'Significant movement in comparatively short-term counselling'. *Journal of Counselling Psychology,* 13 (1), 98-99, 1966.

Grummon, D. L. 'Personality changes as a function of time in persons motivated for therapy'. In C. R. Rogers and R. F. Dymond (eds.). *Psychotherapy and personality change.* Chicago: University of Chicago Press, 1954.

Haase, R. F. 'The relationship of sex and instructional set to the regulation of interpersonal interaction distance in a counselling analogue'. *Journal of Counselling Psychology,* 17, 233-236, 1970.

Halkides, G. 'An investigation of therapeutic success as a function of four variables'. Unpublished Ph.D. thesis, University of Chicago, 1958.

Halmos, P. *The Faith of the Counsellor.* London: Constable Press, 1966.

Halpern, H. M. 'Empathy, similarity and self-satisfaction. *Journal of Consulting Psychology',* 19, 449-452, 1955.

Hamachek, D. E. *Encounters with the self.* New York: Holt, Rinehart and Winston Press, 1971.

Hamilton, G. 'Helping People—The Growth of a Profession'. *Journal of Social Casework,* 29, 296, 1948.

Hanlon, T. F., Hofstaetter, P. R. and O'Connor, J. P. 'Congruence of self and ideal self in relation to personality adjustment'. *Journal of Consulting Psychology,* 18, 215-217, 1954.

Harris, H. I. 'Efficient pyschotherapy for the large outpatient clinic'. *New England Journal of Medicine,* 1, 221, 1939.

Havighurst, R. J., Robinson, M. Z. and Dorr, M. 'The development of the ideal self in childhood and adolescence'. *Journal of Educational Research,* 40, 214-257, 1946.

Hawkins, D. F. 'Estimation of non-response bias'. *Sociological method and research,* 3, 461-485, 1975.

Healy, W., Bronner, A. F., and Bowers, A. M. *The structure and meaning of psychoanalysis.* New York: Knopf, 1930.

Heine, R. W. 'An investigation of the relationship between change in personality from psychotherapy as reported by patients and the factors seen by patients as producing change'. Unpublished Ph.D. thesis, University of Chicago, 1950.

Heine, R. W. and Trosman, H. 'Initial expectations of the doctor-patient interaction as a factor in continuance in psychotherapy'. *Psychiatry,* 23, 275-278, 1960.

Hiler, E. W. 'The sentence completion test as a predictor of continuation in psychotherapy'. *Journal of Consulting Psychology,* 23, 544-549, 1959.

Hilgard, E. 'Human motives and the concept of self'. *American Psychologist,* 4, 374-382, 1949.

Hollenbeck, G. P. 'Conditions and outcomes in the student-parent relationship'. *Journal of Consulting Psychology,* 29 (3), 237-241, 1965.

Hollis, F. *Women in marital conflict.* New York: Family Service Association of America, 1949.

Hood, T. C. and Back, K. W. 'Self-disclosure and the volunteer. A source of bias in laboratory experiments'. *Journal of Personality and Social Psychology,* 17, 130-136, 1971.

Horney, K. *New Ways in Psychoanalysis.* New York: Norton Press, 1939.

Huddleson, J. H. 'Psychotherapy in 200 cases of psychoneurosis'. *Militant Surgeon,* 60, 161, 1927.

Imber, S., Nash, E. and Stone, A. 'Social class and duration of psychotherapy'. *Journal of Clinical Psychology,* 11, 281-284, 1955.

Ingham, H. V. and Love, L. R. *The process of psychotherapy,* New York: McGraw Hill Press, 1954.

Jackson, W. and Carr, A. C. 'Empathic ability in normals and schizophrenics'. *Journal of Abnormal and Social Psychology,* 51, 71-82, 1955.

James, W. *Principles of Psychology.* New York: Holt, Rinehart and Winston Press, 1890.

Janis, E. *Personality and peruasibility.* New Haven: Yale University Press, 1959.

Jourard, S. M. 'A study of self-disclosure'. *Scientific American,* 198, 77-82, 1958.

Jourard, S. M. 'Self-disclosure and other cathexis'. *Journal of Abnormal and Social Psychology*, 59, 428-431, 1959.

Jourard, S. M. and Landsman, M. J. 'Cognition, cathexis, and the 'dyadic effect' in men's self-disclosing behaviour'. *Merrill-Palmer Quarterly of Behaviour and Development*, 6, 178-186, 1960.

Jourard, S. M. and Remy, R. M. 'Perceived Parental Attitudes, the Self and Security'. *Journal of Consulting Psychology*, 19, 364-366, 1955.

Jourard, S. M. and Richman, P. 'Factors in the self-disclosure of college students. *Merrill-Palmer Quarterly of Behaviour and Development*, 9, 141-148, 1963.

Jung, C. G. *Two essays on analytical psychology.* New York: Dodd Mead Press, 1928.

Kagan, N., Krathwohl, D., Goldberg, A. D., Campbell, R. J., Schauble, P. G., Greenberg, B. S., Danish, S. J., Resnikoff, A., Bowes, J., and Bondy, S. B. *Studies in human interaction: Interpersonal process recall stimulated by videotape.* East Lansing: Education Publication Services, 1967.

Katz, P. and Zigler, E. 'Self-image disparity'. *Journal of Personality and Social Psychology*, 5, 186-195, 1967.

Kelly, H. H. and Shapiro, M. M. 'An experiment on conformity to group norms where conformity is detrimental to group achievement'. *American Sociological Review*, 19, 667-677, 1954.

Koestler, A. 'The novelist deals with character'. *Sat. Review of Literature*, 32, 7-8, 1949.

Koffka, K. *Principles of Gestalt Psychology.* New York: Harcourt Brace Press, 1935.

Komarovsky, M. 'Cultural contradictions and sex roles'. *American Journal of Sociology*, 52, 184-189, 1946.

Koren, L., Goetzel, V. and Evans, M. 'The Psychodynamics of Failure in Therapy'. *American Journal of Psychiatry*, 106, 845-850, 1950.

Krasner, L. 'Studies of the conditioning of verbal behaviour'. *Psychological Bulletin*, 55, 148-170, 1958.

Kurland, S. H. 'Length of treatment in a mental hygiene clinic'. *Psychiatric Quarterly Supplement*, 30, 83-90, 1965.

Kurtz, R. R. and Grummon, D. L. 'Different approaches to the measurement of therapist empathy and their relationship to therapy outcomes'. *Journal of Consulting and Clinical Psychology* 39, 1, 106-115, 1972.

Laing, R. D. *The Politics of Experience and The Bird of Paradise.* Harmondsworth, Middlesex: Penguin, 1967.

Landis, C. 'Statistical evaluation of psychotherapeutic methods'. In S.E. Hinsie (ed). *Concepts and problems of psychotherapy,* London: Heineman, 1938.

Langfield, A. W. 'Grid relationship scoring used with a Rep Test modification'. *Psychological Reports,* 21, 19-23, 1967.

Lecky, P. *Self-Consistency: A Theory of Personality.* New York: Island Press, 1945.

Lee, H. *To Kill a Mocking Bird.* Lippincott Press, 1960.

Lesser, W. M. 'The relationship between counselling progress and empathic understanding'. *Journal of Counselling Psychology,* 8, 330-336, 1961.

Levinson, D. G. 'The psychotherapist's contribution to the patient's treatment career'. In Strupp, H. H. and Luborsky, L. (eds). *Research in psychotherapy.* Vol. 2 Washington, D.C.: American Psychological Association, 1962.

Lindzey, G. *Handbook of Social Psychology, Vol. I.* U.S.A.: Addison-Wesley, 1954.

Lipps, T. *Grundtatsachen des Seelenbens,* 1883.

Little, K. B. 'Personal space'. *Journal of Experimental and Social Psychology,* 1, 237-247, 1965.

Litwinski, L. 'Toward the reinstatement of the concept of self'. *British Journal of Psychology,* 42, 246-249, 1951.

Lorr, M., Katz, M. M. and Rubinstein, E. A. 'The prediction of length of stay in psychotherapy'. *Journal of Consulting Psychology,* 22, 321-327, 1958.

Luchins, A. S. 'Restructuring social perceptions. A group psychotherapy technique'. *Journal of Consulting Psychology,* 14, 446-450, 1950.

Luchins, A. S. 'Patients view of the therapist: A training and research device'. *Journal of Consulting Psychology,* 15, 24-31, 1951.

Lundy, R. M. 'Self-perceptions and descriptions of opposite sex sociometric choice'. *Sociometry,* 19, 272-277, 1956.

Maehr, M., Mensing, J. and Nafzger, S. 'Concept of self and the reaction of others'. *Sociometry,* 25, 353-357, 1962.

Manis, M. 'Personal adjustment, assumed similarity to parents, and inferred parental evaluations of the self'. *Journal of Consulting Psychology,* 22, 481-485, 1958.

Mapother, E. 'Discussion of a paper on Thomas S. Good'. *British Journal of Psychology*, 7, 36, 1927.

Marascuile, L. A. and McSweeney, M. *Nonparametric and Distribution Free Methods for the Social Sciences.* Monterey, California: Brooks Cole Press, 1977.

Martin, D. G. *Learning-based Client-Centred Therapy.* Monterey, California: Brooks Cole Press, 1972.

Martin, J. C., Carkhuff, R. R. and Berenson, B. G. 'Process variables in counselling and psychotherapy: a study of counselling and friendship'. *Journal of Counselling Psychology*, 13, 356-359, 1966.

Marzillier, J. S. 'Verbal methods of behaviour change'. *Behaviour Psychotherapy*, 6 (4), 85-90, 1978.

Masserman, J. H. and Carmichael, H. T. 'Diagnosis and Prognosis in Psychiatry with a follow-up study of the results of short-term general hospital therapy of psychiatric cases. *Joural of Mental Science*, 84, 893-946, 1938.

May, R. *Man's Search for Himself.* New York: W. W. Norton & Co, 1953.

McCandless, B. R. *Children: Behaviour and Deviance.* New York: Holt, Rinehart and Winston, 1967.

McCue, M., Goodman, M. and Rosenthal, M. 'Failure to return for treatment: tested and non-tested'. *Journal of Consulting Psychology*, 18, 280, 1954.

McKenna, H., Hofstaetter, P. R. and O'Connor, J. P. 'The concepts of the ideal self and of the friend'. *Journal of Personality*, 24, 262-271, 1956.

McIntyre, C. J. 'Acceptance by others and its relation to acceptance of self and others'. *Journal of Abnormal and Social Psychology*, 47, 624-626, 1952.

Mead, M. *Mind, self and society.* Chicago: University of Chicago Press, 1934.

Medinnus, G. R. 'Q-sort descriptions of five-year-old children by their parents'. *Child Development*, 32, 473-489, 1961.

Meyer, V. and Chesser, E. S. *Behaviour therapy in clinical psychiatry,* Harmondworth, Middlesex: Penguin, 1970.

Miles, H. W. Barrabee, E. L. and Finesinger, J. E. 'Evaluation of psychotherapy'. *Psychosomatic Medicine*, 13, 83, 1951.

Moran, R. A. 'Conceptualisation of Mental Illness and Attitudes towards the Mentally Ill and Ex-Mental Patients'. Unpublished M.A. thesis, U.C. Cork, 1976.

Moser, C. A. and Kalton, G. *Methods in social investigation.* London: Heineman Educational Books Ltd., 1971.

Moustakas, C. *The Self.* New York: Harper and Row, 1956.

Moustakas, C. *The self: explorations in personal growth.* New York: Harper and Row, 1974.

Mowrer, O. H. *Psychotherapy: theory and research.* New York: Ronald Press, 1953.

Mullen, J. and Abeles, N. 'Relationship of liking, empathy, and therapists' experience to outcome of therapy'. *Journal of Counselling Psychology,* 18, 39-45, 1971.

Müller-Freienfels, R. *The Evolution of Modern Psychology.* Yale Univesity Press, 1936.

Munroe, J. S. *Schools of psychoanalytic thought.* New York: Dryden Press, 1955.

Murphy, G. *Personality: a biosocial approach to origin and structure.* New York: Harper and Row, 1947.

Murray, H. A. *Personality in Nature, Society and Culture.* New York: Knopf, 1953.

Musgrave, F. 'The social needs and satisfaction of some young people at school'. *British Journal of Educational Psychology,* 36, 137-149, 1966.

Myers, G. and Myers, M. *The dynamics of human communication.* McGraw Hill, 1976.

Myers, J. K. and Schaffer, L. 'Social stratification and psychiatric practice; a study of an out-patient clinic'. *American Sociological Review,* 19, 307-310, 1954.

Neustatter, W. L. 'Results of 50 cases treated by psychotherapy'. *Lancet,* 1, 796, 1935.

O'Hara, A. P. and Tiedman, D. V. 'The vocational self-concept in adolescence'. *Journal of Counselling Psychology,* 6, 292-301, 1959.

O'Leary, E. and Lenahan, A. *Techniques of Counselling.* Paper read at the National Conference of Guidance Counsellors of Ireland, 1980.

Osterreich, K. *Die Phanomenologie des Ich* Leipzig: 1910.

Omwake, K. T. 'The relationship between acceptance of others shown by three personality inventories'. *Journal of Consulting Psychology,* 18, 443-446, 1954.

Orford, J. *The social psychology of mental disorder.* Pelican, 1976.

Pallone, N. J. 'Self-Interpretive Counselling. A Model for School Guidance' in *Readings in Guidance and Counselling.* New York: Sheed and Ward, 1966.

Patterson, C. H. 'Some notes on behaviour theory, behaviour therapy and behavioural counselling'. *The Counselling Psychologist* 1 (4), 44-56, 1969.

Patterson, C. H. *Relationship Counselling and Psychotherapy.* New York: Harper and Row, 1974.

Payne, J., Drummond, A. W. and Lunghi, M. 'Changes in the self-concepts of school-leavers who participated in an Arctic Expedition'. *British Journal of Educational Psychology,* 40, 211-216, 1970.

Phillips, E. L. 'Attitudes towards self and others: a brief questionnaire report'. *Journal of Consulting Psychology,* 15, 79-81, 1951.

Polansky, N. A. 'On duplicity in the interview'. *American Journal of Orthopsychiatry,* 37, 568-580, 1967.

Powell, J. *Why am I afraid to tell you who I am?* Wiles, Illinois: Argus, 1969.

Raimy, V. C. 'Self-reference in counselling interviews'. *Journal of Consulting Psychology,* 12, 153-163, 1948.

Raskin, N. *Studies on psychotherapeutic orientation: ideology in practice.* A.A.P. Psychotherapy Research Monographs, Orlando, Florida: American Academy of Psychotherapists, 1974.

Rausch, H. L. and Bordin, E. S. 'Warmth in Personality Development and in Psychotherapy'. *Psychiatry,* 20, 351-363, 1957.

Redlich, F. C. and Hollingshead, A. B. 'Social structure and psychiatric treatment'. *American Journal of Psychiatry,* 109, 729-734, 1953.

Reik, T. *Listening with the Third Ear.* New York: Ferrar Strauss, 1949.

Robinson, H. A., Redlick, F. C. and Myers, J. K. 'Social structure and psychiatric treatment'. *American Journal of Orthopsychiatry,* 24, 307-316, 1954.

Rogers, C. R. 'The attitude and orientation of the counsellor'. *Journal of Consulting Psychology,* 13, 82-94, 1949.

Rogers, C. R. 'A process conception of psychotherapy'. *American Psychologist,* 13, 142-149, 1958.

Rogers, C. R. *Client-centred Therapy.* New York: Houghton-Mifflin, 1951.

Rogers, C. R. 'Changes in the maturity of behaviour as related to therapy'. In C. R. Rogers and F. Dymond (eds.) *Psychotherapy and personality change*. Chicago: Uni. of Chicago Press, 1954.

Rogers, C. R. 'Persons or science: a philosophical question. *American Psychologist*, 10, 267, 1965.

Rogers, C. R. 'The necessary and sufficient conditions of therapeutic personality change'. *Journal of Consulting Psychology*, 21, 95-103, 1957.

Rogers, C. R. *On Becoming a Person*. Boston: Houghton-Mifflin, 1961.

Rogers, C. R. 'The interpersonal relationship'. *Harvard Educational Review*, 32, 416-429, 1962.

Rogers, C. R. 'The therapeutic relationship: recent theory and research'. *Australian Journal of Psychology*, 17, 95-108, 1963.

Rogers, C. R. *The therapeutic relationship and its impact: A study of psychotherapy with schizophrenics*. Madison, Wisconson: 1967.

Rogers, C. R. *Freedom to learn*. Columbus, Ohio: Charles Merrill, 1971.

Rogers, C. R. and Dymond, R. F. *Psychotherapy and Personality Change*. Chicago: University of Chicago Press, 1954.

Rosenberg, M. *Society and the Adolescent Self-Image*. Princeton, N.J.: Princeton University Press, 1965.

Rosenthal, D. and Frank, J. D. 'Psychotherapy and the placebo effect'. *Psychological Bulletin*, 53, 294-302, 1956.

Rosenthal, D. and Frank, J. D. 'The fate of psychiatric clinic outpatients assigned to psychotherapy'. *Journal of Nervous and Mental Disorders*, 127, 330-343, 1958.

Rubinstein, E. A. and Lorr, M. 'A comparison of terminators and remainers in outpatient psychotherapy'. *Journal of Clinical Psychology*, 12, 345-349, 1956.

Rycroft, C. *A Critical Dictionary of Psychoanalysis*. London: Nelson Press, 1968.

Sander, K., Tausch, R., Bastine, R. and Nagel, K. 'Die auswirkung experimenteller anderungen des pschotherapeutenuerhaltens auf Kleinten in psychotherapeutischen gesprachen'. (In manuskript), 1968.

Schaffer, L. and Myers, J. K. 'Psychotherapy and social stratification: an empirical study of practice in a psychiatric outpatient clinic'. *Psychiatry*, 17, 83-93, 1954.

Scheffe, H. *The Analysis of Variance*. New York: Wiley Press, 1959.

Seeman, J. and Raskin, N. J. 'Research perspective in client-centred therapy'. In Mowrer, O.H. (ed). *Psychotherapy: theory and research.* New York: Ronald Press, 1953.

Shaw, C. R. *The Jack-Roller.* Chicago: University of Chicago Press, 1930.

Shaw, M. E. and Wright, J. M. *Scales for the Measurement of Attitudes.* New York: McGraw Hill, 1967.

Sheerer, E. T. 'An analysis of the relationship between acceptance of and respect for self and acceptance of and respect for others in 10 counselling cases'. *Journal of Consulting Psychology,* 13, 169-175, 1949.

Shertzer, B. and Shelley, C. *Fundamentals of Counselling.* Boston, 1974.

Shranger, J. S. 'Responses to evaluation as a function of initial self-perceptions'. *Psychological Bulletin,* 1975, 82, 581-589, 1975.

Snelbecker, G. E. 'Factors influencing college students perceptions of psychotherapists in a laboratory analog'. Unpublished Ph.D. thesis, Cornell University, 1961.

Snelbecker, G. E. 'Influence of therapeutic techniques on college students perceptions of therapists'. *Journal of Consulting Psychology,* 31 (6), 614-618, 1967.

Snyder, W. U. 'Warmth in nondirective counselling'. *Journal of Abnormal and Social Psychology.* 41, 491-495, 1946.

Sommer, R. 'Studies in personal space'. *Sociometry,* 22, 247-260, 1959.

Speisman, J. 'Depth of interpretation and verbal resistance in psychotherapy'. *Journal of Consulting Psychology,* 23, 93-99, 1959.

Standal, S. 'The need for positive regard. A contribution to client-centred theory'. University of Chicago. Unpublished Ph.D. thesis, 1954.

Stock, D. 'An investigation into the interrelations between the self-concept and feelings directed toward other persons and groups'. *Journal of Consulting Psychology,* 13, 176-180, 1949.

Stotland, E. and Dunn, R. E. 'Empathy, self-esteem and birth order'. *Journal of Abnormal and Social Psychology,* 66, 532-540, 1963.

Stranger, J. S. 'Responses to evaluation as a function of initial self-perceptions'. *Psychological Bulletin,* 82, 581-589, 1975.

Strickland, B. and Crowne, D. 'Need for approval and the premature terminator'. *Journal of Consulting Psychology,* 27, 95-101, 1963.

Suinn, R. M. 'The relationship between self-acceptance and acceptance of others'. *Journal of Abnormal and Social Psychology,* 63, 37-42, 1961.

Sullivan, H. S. *Conceptions of Modern Psychiatry.* Washington, D.C.: White Psychiatric Foundation, 1947.
Sullivan, H. S. *The Interpersonal Theory of Psychiatry.* New York: Norton Press, 1953.

Tagiuri, R. 'Social preference and its perception. In Tagiuri, R. and Petrullo, L. *Person Perception and Interpersonal Behaviour.* Stanford California: Stanford University Press, 1958.
Tagiuri, R., Blake, R. and Bruner, J. S. 'Some determinants of the perception of positive and negative feelings in others'. *Journal of Abnormal and Social Psychology,* 48, 585-592, 1953.
Tarachow, S. *An introduction to psychotherapy.* New York: International Universities Press, 1963.
Tausch, R. *Personal Communication from R. Tausch to C. Rogers,* 1973.
Tausch, R., Bastine, R., Bommert, H., Minsel, W. R. and Nickel, H. 'Untersuchung der Auswirkung unter Prozesse Klientenzentrierter Gesprachpsychotherapie'. *Zeitschrift fur Klinische Psychologie,* 1 (3), 232-250, 1972.
Tausch, R., Eppel, H., Filtkan, B. and Minsel, R. 'Variablen and zusanumehange in der gesprachspsychotherapie'. *Zeitschrift fur Psychologie,* 176, 93-102, 1969.
Telschow, E. *The role of the group leader in nondirective group psychotherapy.* Ed. D. project, Teachers College, Columbia University, 1950.
Thomas, E. and Burdick, H. 'Self-esteem and Defense Preference as related to social behaviour'. (Unpublished manuscript), University of Michigan, 1954.
Thornton, B. M. 'Dimensions of perceived relationship as related to marital adjustment'. Unpublished Master's thesis, Auburn University, 1960.
Titchener, E. B. *An Outline of Psychology.* Macmillan Press, 1896.
Titchener, E. B. 'A note on the consciousness of self'. *American Journal of Psychology,* 22, 540-552, 1911.
Tolman, R. and Meyer, M. 'Who returns to the clinic for more therapy'. *Mental Hygiene,* 41, 497-506, 1957.
Truax, C. B. *A scale for the measurement of accurate empathy.* Discussion paper. No. 20. University of Wisconsin Press, 1961.
Truax, C. B. 'A tentative scale for the measurement of unconditional positive regard'. *Psychiatric Institute Bulletin,* Wisconsin, 2, 1, 1962.

Truax, C. B. 'Effective Ingredients in Psychotherapy. An Approach to unravelling the patient-therapist interaction'. *Journal of Counselling Psychology,* 10, 256-263, 1963.

Truax, C. B. *A scale for the rating of Accurate Empathy in the Therapeutic Relationship and it's Impacts.* University of Wisconsin Press, 1967.

Truax, C. B. and Carkhuff, P. R. 'Client and therapist transparency in the psychotherapeutic encounter'. *Journal of Counselling Psychology,* 12, 3-9, 1965.

Truax, C. B. and Carkhuff, R. R. 'The experimental manipulation of therapeutic conditions'. *Journal of Consulting Psychology,* 29, 119-124, 1965.

Truax, C. B. and Carkhuff, R. R. *Toward Effective Counselling and Psychotherapy.* Chicago: Aldine, 1967.

Truax, C. B. Carkhuff, R. R. and Kodman, F. 'Relationships between therapist-offered conditions and patient change in group psychotherapy'. *Journal of Clinical Psychology,* 21, 327-329, 1965.

Truax, C. B. and Mitchell, K. 'Research on certain therapist interpersonal skills in relation to process and outcome'. In Bergin A. and Garfield S. (eds). *Handbook of Psychotherapy and Behaviour Change.* Wiley Press, 1971.

Truax, C. B. and Wargo, D. G. 'Antecedents to outcome in group psychotherapy with outpatients: Effects of therapeutic conditions, alternate sessions, vicarious therapy pre-training and patient self-exploration'. *Journal of Consulting and Clinical Psychology,* 33, 1967.

Truax, C. B., Wargo, D. G., Frank, J. D., Imber, S. D., Battle, C. C., Hoen-Saric, R., Nash, E. N. and Stone, A. R. 'Therapist empathy, genuineness and warmth and patient therapeutic outcome'. *Journal of Consulting Psychology,* 30, 395-401, 1966.

Tuckman, B. W. 'Interpersonal probing and revealing and systems of integrative complexity'. *Journal of Personality,* 3, 655-664, 1966.

Turner, R. H. and Vanderlippe, R. 'Self-ideal congruence as an index of adjustment'. *Journal of Abnormal and Social Psychology,* 57, 202-206, 1958.

Tyler, L. E. *The Work of the Counsellor.* New York: Appleton-Century-Crofts, Inc., 1953.

Ullman, L. and Krasner, L. *A psychological approach to abnormal behaviour.* New York: Prentice-Hall, Inc., 1975.

Van der Veen, F. *Dimensions of client and therapist behaviour in relation to outcome.* Proceedings of the 73rd annual convention of the American Psychological Association. Washington, D.C., 1965.

Videbeck, R. 'Self-conception and the reaction of others'. *Sociometry,* 23, 351-359, 1960.

Vondracek, S. and Vondracek, F. 'The manipulation and measurement of self-disclosure in preadolescents'. *Merrill-Palmer Quarterly,* 17, 51-58, 1971.

Wallis, D. *Some Pressing Problems for Research in Vocational Guidance.* Paper to the Welsh Branch of the British Psychological Society. November, 1978.

Walster, E. 'The effect of self-esteem on romantic liking'. *Journal of Experimental and Social Psychology,* 1, 184-197, 1965.

Weiner, I. *Principles of Psychotherapy.* New York: Wiley and Sons, 1975.

Wenger, P. 'Uber weitere Ergebnisse der Psychotherapie in Rahmen einer Medizinischen Poliklinik'. *Wien. Med. Wchmschr,* 84, 320, 1934.

White, A., Fichtenbaun, L. and Dollard, J. 'Measure for predicting dropping out of psychotherapy'. *Journal of Consulting Psychology,* 28, 326-332, 1964.

Winder, A. E. and Hersko, M. 'The effect of social class on length and type of psychotherapy in a Veterans Administration mental hygiene clinic'. *Journal of Clinical Psychology,* 11, 77-79, 1955.

Wolberg, L. R. *The Technique of Psychotherapy.* New York: Grune and Stratton, Inc., 1954 (1st ed.), 1967 (2nd ed).

Wolf, R. and Murray, H. A. 'An experiment in judging personalities'. *Journal of Psychology,* 3, 345-365, 1947.

Wundt, W. *Human and Animal Psychology.* London, 1894.

Wylie, R. *The Self Concept: A Critical Survey of Pertinent Research Literature.* Lincoln: University of Nebraska Press, 1961.

Yaskin, J. C. 'The psychoneuroses and neuroses: a review of 100 cases with special reference to treatment and end results'. *American Journal of Psychiatry,* 93, 107, 1936.

Ziller, R. C. *The Social Self.* New York: Pergamon Press, 1973.

Index

NOTES

NOTES

NOTES